Advance Reviews For "Why Should Someone Do Business With You?"

"It's great—filled with pointed and entertaining examples from the real world. Geist's poignant questions lead the reader on a very solid 'reality check' of their own. At the same time the book leads the reader to the appropriate 'bottomline' oriented focus and action plan that can't miss."
Michael Van de Kamp, Vice President, American Medical Security

" 'Why Should Someone Do Business With You...' is the most valuable resource for taking care of your business to hit the bookstores in a long, long time. Short on theory, long on practicality, Geist has filled every page with new insights and implementable suggestions for everything from marketing and customer service to staff training and leadership skills. Best of all are the 21 questions that follow each section—they provide a built-in 'opener' for staff training sessions."
Phil Brown, General Manager, Growmark Inc.

"Geist has synthesized what doing business in our rapidly changing world is all about. His clear and focused approach enables the reader to understand the parameters of change, the opportunities it creates and how-to transform it into energy. Geist's very practical, thought-provoking information takes the mystery out of marketing today, so all business people, big or small can feel very comfortable in their role—and actually do it! The Canadian Home Builders' Association recommends this book highly as an indispensable resource for success, especially to our many new home builder and renovator members who own small businesses."
John Kenward, Chief Operating Officer, Canadian Home Builders' Association

" 'Why Should Someone Do Business With You...Rather Than Someone Else?' is perfectly timed due to the competitive environment and changes that have taken place in virtually every business in North America. This book includes all the important ingredients that are required for a business to be successful including leadership, vision, technology, research, marketing, customer service and training. The series of questions at the end of each section, along with the numerous quotes will assist and stimulate the reader."
Norm Latowsky, Vice Chairman, Dylex Ltd.

" 'Why Should Someone Do Business With You…' provides a blueprint to change. To transform an organization in order to enhance its customer satisfaction and increase their loyalty, demands transformation and changed behavior from the service givers involved. Geist's practical approach helps you make that vital transformation."
Ed Robinson, President & CEO, Aetna Health Management

"Bravo! I think Sam Geist has fulfilled his mandate, and along the way, has introduced a very novel approach to involving the reader in a truly 'interactive' experience. It is rare to find a book today that actually puts you in the position of being able to analyze the areas that you can improve on to make your business an ongoing success. It's like having your own personal consultant available at your fingertips. This book is a must for anyone who either runs their own business, or who works in a business that deals with the public in any capacity. I will recommend it to my own staff as an excellent way of helping to keep them focused on the most important goal of our business; making sure that our clients want to continue to do business with us rather than someone else."
Dr. Stephen Simms, Millenium Communications Inc.

"In today's competitive marketplace, a clear and easy-to-follow guide to differentiate yourself, your people, your organization from your competitors is critical. 'Why Should Someone Do Business With You…' is such a guide. Not only does Geist help you reach your goal, he provides encouragement along the way with real life experiences, comments from those who have traveled a similar route and challenging questions to answer. You'll be delighted at the new view when you arrive at your destination!"
Keith Van Beek, President, Toys R Us

"In a world of increasing consumer expectations and brutal competition, Sam Geist has delivered THE textbook of business management for the end of this decade and beyond. This book is informative, hard-hitting and delivers a timely message. It's a must-read for every marketer. I love it."
Elena Opasini, Editor, Hardware & Home Centre Magazine

"What a captivating manuscript! I have read many business-related books over the years, and rarely have any managed to rivet my attention and interest as much as Sam Geist's did. His 'interactive' book, with the 21 questions at the end of each chapter compel the reader to seriously think about what he/she is doing.

Considering that ICPB is going through an intense culture change, I found this book provided me with a lot of positive insights into matters which our management must take under advisement now. Had I not read it, these matters would have been handled, but much, much too late. 'Why Should...', is likely intended for 'For-Profit' organizations. However, so many aspects can be applied to 'Not-for-Profit' organizations that I have no hesitation in recommending it to them as well. Timely and very well-thought out."
Jean-Claude Cloutier, President, Insurance Crime Prevention Bureau

"Sam writes like he speaks—to the point, with meaningful examples, and a challenge to answer the questions for yourself. I've heard him motivate thousands of our dealers to answer 'Why Should Someone Do Business With Me?' "
James B. Mathews, Vice President-Corporate Marketing,
Hunter Douglas Window Fashions

"Sam Geist has planted wonderful seeds again. This book is overflowing with the fruit of the marvelous seeds of his ideas on marketing that is extraordinary. You will use this material in a thousand new ways."
Dottie Walters, President, Walters International Speakers Bureau

"A must-read for everyone in business today—whether you sell or manufacture or distribute products or offer services. 'Why Should Someone Do Business With You...' inspires you to take charge of your situation and then provides you with the specific tools to do just that. Geist clearly illustrates how you can create new opportunities by understanding the changing needs and wants of your market. His pointed questions (and there are hundreds) challenge you to re-view—to re-new and move ahead."
William E. Ardell, former President & CEO, Southam Inc.

WHY?

SHOULD SOMEONE DO BUSINESS WITH YOU...

RATHER THAN SOMEONE ELSE

SAM GEIST

ADDINGTON &
WENTWORTH INC.

TORONTO, ONTARIO
CANADA

NAPLES, FLORIDA
UNITED STATES

Published simultaneously in Canada and in the United States by Addington & Wentworth, Inc.

For information address:

Addington & Wentworth, Inc.
327 Renfrew Drive, Suite 301
Markham, ON   CANADA L3R 9S8
(905) 475-1022

First Edition
Second Printing

Library of Congress Catalogue Card Number: 97-70904

Canadian Cataloguing in Publication Data:

Geist, Sam, 1945-

"WHY SHOULD SOMEONE DO BUSINESS WITH YOU...RATHER THAN SOMEONE ELSE?": new perspectives and differentiating strategies to get and keep customers, to increase staff productivity and business profitability

Includes index

ISBN 1-896984-00-2

1. Industrial management   2. Business   3. Marketing   I Title

HF5351.G44 1997   658   C97-900202-8

Dedication

To the business men and women everywhere who realize that a business without customers—*isn't* and therefore demonstrate their commitment to get and keep customers, in everything they do.

Acknowledgments

To Michelle Avoledo for her tireless hours of inputting, re-inputting and re-re-inputting, and her faith that this book would indeed, one day, be done.

To all the manuscript readers who generously offered insights, suggestions, criticism and encouragement—Len Kubas, Dr. Larry Steinmetz, Keith Van Beek, Fraser McAllan and Keith Talbot.

To Terry Kounelas for his enthusiasm, his patience and his creative and production skills.

To my son Michael, for his expert proofing, wise observations, invaluable insights and exacting standards which have immeasurably enhanced the final version.

To June Rodgers for her careful editing and her astute comments.

To my children Michael, Allison, Aaron, Rebecca and Josh for their love, continued support, enthusiasm and belief in this lengthy project.

And finally, my deep gratitude to my wife Rene for her years of encouragement and unfailing support in this and all our other endeavors. Without her dedicated effort this book would not be a reality.

CONTENTS

Preface

It is amazing how the vista changes when you adjust your viewing platform. As owner and operator of a retail sporting goods organization that grew by leaps and bounds in the 1970s, I thought I knew everything. After all I was a successful retailer. I overcame the same challenges the other retailers overcame and took the same Maalox they took.

When in the early 1980s, I moved from retailing to advertising and marketing, I was amazed at how different the scene appeared. It didn't take long before I, once again, thought I knew everything. After all, I ran a successful advertising agency. I overcame the same challenges the other agency people overcame and took the same Zantac they took.

As the advertising and marketing evolved into consulting and speaking, the view changed once again. I finally realized two things. *First*, I didn't know everything. No one knows everything. *Second*, the view changes dramatically

> *Learning is movement from moment to moment.*
> Jiddu Krishnamurti

when you adjust your viewing platform. Each of us needs to observe from as many different viewing platforms as we can and then act on what we've discovered. It's how we learn. It's how we grow. It's how we create our future.

I have made it my business, quite literally, to share the remarkable vistas I have discovered ever since.

I ask a lot of questions. It provides me with the information I need. It provides me and whoever is answering with a new viewing platform.

Questions challenge. Questions push. Questions prompt review. They call out for action. They motivate change.

When I ask, ***"Why should someone do business with you...rather than someone else?"*** at the start of my seminars, I see the wheels begin to turn in participants' minds.

It's the toughest, most evaded question I know. It's also the question we must all face every day in every business situation. We're quick to talk about our quality — our service — our operations — our staff, but we're slow to face this question head-on and determine what it is about our quality, our service, our operations, our staff that makes us different, makes us special, makes someone want to do business with us, rather than someone else.

Seminar participants want answers. They're looking for solutions. When the mega-bookstores feature 4,400 different business titles on their shelves, you know everyone is looking for answers.

This book asks a lot of questions, the most important being, ***"Why should someone do business with you...rather than someone else?"*** The questions will start your wheels turning. They'll prompt you to search for new viewing platforms, discover new possibilities, open exciting options, find new answers, no matter what your business may be. Today's global village, which we call home, with its glut of products and services, its gross margin erosion, its disintegration of trust, demands positive response, cries out for action.

"Why Should Someone Do Business With You... Rather Than Someone Else?"

There is no one answer to this question — there are many. Each section of this book concentrates on raising issues, asking questions and providing insights and recommendations in a specific area.

Part one examines our rapidly changing environment. Knowing what is changing and understanding the forces that precipitate change and their parameters enables you to consider my questions from new perspectives, ask intuitive questions of your own and search for your own appropriate answers to "why?"

Part two turns its attention to you and your customers — how to create better understanding, more profitable relationships. Knowing your customers well assists you to honestly answer *"Why should someone do business with you...rather than someone else?"* as well as a host of other questions that are asked. Your answers are integral to your business plan.

Part three provides a bold and exciting perspective on that age old subject — marketing. Viable suggestions, innovative options, intrusive questions and your own answers to those questions, encourage you to re-examine your marketing strategies and beneficially re-new them.

Part four looks at providing the elusive customer service we all seek. It outlines the tenets of heroic service in a wide variety of circumstances and asks questions you may never have considered before in your quest to give customers what they really want.

Part five examines one of the most soul-searching questions in the book — who works for you — ambassadors or assassins — and why? Reliable tools and techniques are offered to enable you to actualize a productive and satisfied workforce.

Part six focuses on the importance of owning a vision — and the necessity of moving it to reality. Analysis of other organizations' visions and the implications of the strategic questions asked, assist you to develop an action-oriented vision for your organization.

Part seven concentrates on the centrality of your role as a leader. It asks you to question and re-define your position, your skills, your power, your goals and develop real answers to ***"Why should someone do business with you...rather than someone else?"***

By the conclusion of the book you will find that the information included, the experiences of others, the wise words and quotes of those who know, the intrusive questions, will have assisted to strengthen and mobilize your resources — to take action — to make a difference — to create your own future.

Look through the quotes, peruse the questions at the end of each section before you begin. Read with a pencil in hand. Jot down ideas as they come to you. Make resolutions. Answer the questions. They are not rhetorical. They have been included to encourage you to think about your business in new ways, to adopt different vantage points than you did before. Consider what you can do to change, to improve, to grow. Regard the triumphs of the organizations highlighted as examples of achievement, realizing at the same time that organizations, like individuals are not perfect. We can, however, certainly learn from and adapt their successes to our own situation.

To further broaden your viewing platform, 21 questions wait at the conclusion of each section for your response. Why 21? To remember that we must ask and honestly answer tough questions to be in business in the 21st Century.

Share the questions with colleagues, associates, staff. Add questions of your own *(space has been provided)*. Your answers will instigate more questions as they provide new views, new vistas. Ask yourself the questions again when you've completed the entire book. Make an appointment with yourself to consider the questions yet again in six months. You'll find your answers change, just as your situation and your marketplace change. Asking and answering *(and planning and changing)* are the lifeblood of a business. It is what keeps your business young and healthy and vibrant and sharp.

Never stop asking. Never stop answering, *"Why should someone do business with you...rather than someone else?"* Start now. **ASK. ANSWER. PLAN. CHANGE.**

The search to discover *"Why should someone do business with you...rather than someone else?"* begins with the marketplace, its changing challenges, the changing lifestyles and workstyles of its inhabitants, your customers, and the role of changing technology. It concludes with the recognition that a response is required. Ten action steps to assist in making that response — and answer *"Why should someone do business with you... rather than someone else?"* are included in part one.

CHANGE OR DECAY

What has changed?

What is different today than it was 10 years ago, last year, last week, yesterday?

Almost everything.

Change, the scariest word in the English language now confronts us more audaciously than at any time since the Industrial Revolution.

Change alters business environments and personal lifestyles. It transforms established realities. It mandates innovation, creates new expectations. It demands action. Change or be left behind. Change or become extinct. Change or decay! The choice is not whether, it is when. Change before you must.

> ***It's easier to make change happen when there's a burning platform — a crisis — that is obvious to everyone.***
>
> Larry Bossidy, CEO
> AlliedSignal
> *Chief Executive*

To maintain a leadership position, organizations today must get better, *faster.* Their strategic questioning, visionizing, planning, thinking are all being played out in the bowels of change. They must ask questions and seek answers

> *A great wind is blowing, and that gives you either imagination or a headache. (Referring to the changing times)*
>
> Catherine the Great, (1729-96)
> Empress of Russia
> Correspondence with
> Baron F. M. Grimm

applicable for today. They must also ask questions and seek new and different answers applicable for tomorrow, because with change moving the marketplace so rapidly, tomorrow's answers are no less important than today's.

What's changed? Our habits — how we live — what we eat — where we spend — how we communicate. *What's changed?* Our workplace — how and where and when we work.

Emerging technologies, our information base, our global reach have all changed and continue to change.

> *Consumer spending is the economic engine.*
>
> Sam Geist

At every level, in every industry, change produces far-reaching rippling effects that require acknowledgment and response. When up to 70 percent of the North American G.D.P. (Gross Domestic Product) is comprised of consumer spending, it behooves us to know where we are spending, on what, when, and why, because the ramifications of these answers have enormous implications.

On December 31, 1996, *USA Today* published its "What's In/What's Out" List for 1997. Included among its predictions are: "Temping" is in — "Permanent jobs" are out; "Outsourcing" is in — "Vertical Integration" is out; "Cybershopping" is in — "The mall" is out; "Caffeinated water" is in — "Evian water" is out; "E-junk mail" is in — "Junk faxes" are out.

How do those predictions affect you as a consumer? as a marketer?

By being acutely aware of the changes that have occurred we can, as individuals, as leaders, as organizations, begin to develop a future-focused action plan. One that evolves in sync with the times.

The future never just happened. It was created.

Will Durant (1885-1981) and
Ariel Durant (1898-1981), historians and writers
The Lessons of History

OUR CHANGING HABITS

We have always been the agent and the product of change. Population increases, changing demographics, family diversity have all affected and been effected by the very situations they create.

Looking in our rear-view mirror we clearly see the changes the basic family unit has undergone in the last few years. Not only is it different in size, but the family structure itself has also radically and probably irreversibly changed.

The physical size of the traditional family, *(a 3.7 person unit, consisting of mother, father and children)*, "Father Knows Best" style has shrunk appreciably to 3.1 persons.

Single parent *(mother or father)* families with children are common, as are families without children, same-sex and three generation families living in the same house. Families with two working parents and latch-key children are as prevalent as singles living together. As reported in *The Futurist* (September '95) single-person households are one of the three most-common household types and could by the year 2005 become the most common.

Several reports from the U.S. Census Bureau featured in *U.S. News and World Report* (December '94) specify the diverse experiences of growing up in America. More than 30 million children are being raised by a single parent, step-parents, half siblings or grandparents. Twenty-seven percent are being raised by a lone parent, twice as many as in 1970. And for the first time in history, the lone parent is as likely to have never been married, as divorced. Finally, 54 percent of all kids under six live in families where both parents or the sole parent work.

These different households represent different needs, demands and consumer spending.

As a marketer, are you aware of your target market's living styles, their needs and demands? Are you addressing them? As the marketplace evolves, do you know what their emerging needs and demands will be? Do you know how you will address them?

These questions require response. They demand consideration so that you can determine *"Why should someone do business with you...rather than someone else?"*

Consider emerging trends and how they affect the marketplace in general and your target market(s) in particular.

With ears tuned acutely to the marketplace, futurists predict. They "see" the marketplace of tomorrow with its challenges and opportunities. Faith Popcorn predicted "cocooning" and "small gratifications" and "cashing out" in *The Popcorn Report*.

David Foot, a professor at University of Toronto together with Daniel Stoffman used the Canadian demographic shift perspective to explain away the growing interest in golf and the declining interest in ice hockey in *Boom, Bust & Echo*.

Astute marketers can be futurists, too, if they stay close to their customers. Real close. By knowing what "makes your customers tick," you hold the key to providing what your customers want and need throughout their life cycles.

Consider these hot trends. They are only an indication of what affects you and your market. Determine how you as a consumer are influenced while you as a marketer can create an opportunity.

As interest in personal well-being peaks, health, health clubs, fitness and beauty magazines, health stores, holistic centers, exercise clubs, diet groups, vitamins, spas, home exercisers flourish.

The demand for personalized services and personalized products curves upward with the interest in good health. They offer the provider a competitive advantage.

Find your competitive niche. Exploit it.

> *America is a consumer culture, and when we change what we buy — and how we buy it — we'll change who we are.*
>
> Faith Popcorn, futurist and author,
> *The Popcorn Report*

The hefty cost of "Saturday night out," together with the increased accessibility of video stores and the Internet have made staying at home, to relax with a movie or surf the Net a most acceptable evening's entertainment to the younger generation.

To accommodate "stay-at-homes," delivery of everything from pizza to chicken to gourmet is available. A battle for "stomach share" rages.

Record spending continues on eating away-from-home whether it's delivered or eaten out. In Canada, 32 percent of the food budget is spent outside the home. In the United States, as reported in *USA Today*, fast food was being eaten to the tune of $97 billion in 1995, teenage boys being far and away the biggest fast-food consumers. It is interesting that while the talk is for healthy, lean cuisine, the reverse appears to be the case when eating. The most popular fast food is the "nastiest" — loaded with calories, cheese and fat. But will it last? Fast-food watchers are now talking about "wraps"—hand-held burrito-like entrees stuffed with almost any food you can think of — expected to exceed $500 million in sales in 1997. **How is this trend affecting you and your business?**

> *We're talking coronary on a crust. (Referring to the calories, salt and saturated fat in Pizza Hut's Triple Decker Pizza.)*
>
> Jayne Hurley, senior nutritionist
> Center for Science in the Public Interest
> *USA Today*

The Boomers, that 87.8 million person blip in North American society, are looking for not-so-fast food, in a relaxed atmosphere where they can enjoy a family meal with their kids, with wine, without breaking the bank. As the demand grows, sales increases for casual dining restaurants, dubbed BATH (Better Alternatives To Home) reach double digits. At least there's no dishes to wash!

The battle for stomach share doesn't end there. Traditional

grocery stores that waged war with food discounters, such as Price Club/Costco and Sam's Warehouse Club, have another fight on their hands. Many gourmet shops, butchers, restaurants and sandwich shops, offer grocery shopping via computer modem. The Internet, as well, gives access to a vast eating public. For people hard pressed to find the time to shop in person, these latest conveniences may be just the solution.

I recently overheard an interesting perspective on new opportunity: "Today's customers don't buy groceries, they buy the answers to that age-old question, 'What's for dinner?' " Absolutely true!

As a marketer, your challenge and your opportunity lies in fulfilling the changing quest for sustenance— for solutions to desires.

Ironically, at a time when disposal income has declined in North America, opportunities to spend it has reached an all-time high. Traditional malls are ready to take your hard-earned dollar, as are discount stores, including the giant retailers, off-price outlet malls, strip malls and small boutiques. Also available for your shopping pleasure, should you wish to indulge, are catalogs (ever growing), teleshopping, computer shopping and Internet shopping.

My son, Michael and daughter-in-law, Allison, living in New Jersey, wanted to send

53 percent of American shoppers are shopping less — not to save money but to save time. On average shoppers devote three hours a week to shopping— two for food and necessities; one for apparel and other goods.

Kurt Salmon Associates Consumer Survey
Discount Store News

flowers to his sister, in Chicago. Browsing through the Internet, Michael found a florist in Arizona, who advertised, with photos, just the arrangement they wanted to send — sunflowers in a ceramic vase. The transaction was completed in minutes on the Net. The flowers arrived the next day to Rebecca's delight. A busy customer has choice.

Marketers have been warned that today's customers are looking for "value-added" experiences — more than just a pleasant outing, good prices and appropriate service. They're looking for entertainment, fun, solutions, an experience to remember. And the winners of today's battle for market share are those who will give more than just a single reason to come, to use, to try, to buy.

> *Shopping is a form of entertainment.*
>
> Leonard Riggio, CEO
> Barnes & Noble
> *Fortune*

OUR CHANGING WORKPLACE

The gradual disappearance of traditional family roles, the disappearance of apron-clad mom waving good-bye at the doorstep is mirrored in the transformation occurring in the workplace — in the offices, factories and businesses across the country.

Two particular developments have had tremendous impact — technological evolution and economic uncertainty. Together, they have created many near-empty offices, receptionless reception areas, voice mail, computer-run factories and department stores devoid of staff.

These cataclysmic phenomena have left in their wake challenges and new opportunities. Aided by rapidly developing communications technology and accelerated by industrial restructuring, innovative cottage industries have sprung up to service the rapidly growing number of home offices. Conceived to address these new needs and demands, trade shows, trade magazines and consultants dot the landscape. This work style, fortified by reduced financial risk and lower stress, is flourishing.

It has even acquired an acronym of its own, SOHO (Small Office — Home Office), *a sure sign of success.* Demonstrating its aggressive entrepreneurship, Kinkos wasted no time in becoming the resource of choice, offering printing, computer facilities, video conferencing capabilities to home office businesses, 24 hours a day. It is capitalizing on change.

Employees left behind in large corporations, working harder, faster and trying to accomplish what two or three or four employees previously achieved, also have their needs. They are "time poor." They spend to save time. Evidence of their spending habits grow, and business opportunities along with it.

Spiegel's, the granddaddy of American catalogs, got my business recently because it understood how time constrained I am. I wanted to send a client in Philadelphia a thank-you gift. Chose a clock from its catalog. Called its 1-800 number at 11 pm to place the order from Canada. No problem. It offers 24-hour service. The telephone representative took my credit card number and a few days later my client received the package. No running to the mall as it's closing. No hassle.

Not to be outdone by what he felt was impressive service, my son Michael remarked that MacWarehouse, a computer retailer, offers next day country-wide delivery on orders received by midnight.

My appliance repairman, Gerry Van Hoorn, increased his hours to fit his customers' needs. Not home 'til 9 p.m.? Don't worry. Home only on the weekends? Not a concern. He arrives when it's convenient for us, *his customers*.

Take a look at today's changing workplace. Contemplate tomorrow's workplace. Anticipate arising needs. Evaluate emerging opportunities. Ask ***"Why should somebody do business with you...rather than someone else today?"*** Ask **"What can you do to encourage someone to do business with you tomorrow?"**

OUR CHANGING TECHNOLOGY

Our never ending search to make our existence easier, our personal environment more comfortable, our business environment more productive, has been given a catapulting jolt. What a short while ago seemed fantastic is today virtual reality. Rudy Puryear, senior information technology strategist for Andersen Consulting succinctly clarified its mighty grasp when he said, "Technology right now is blowing away barriers of time, distance and form in ways we've never seen before." Technology has always changed how we live, how we conduct our business and our financial affairs, even how we entertain ourselves — it's just never done it so fast. We may fear the speed, but we respect the power.

Technology that defines our ability to communicate has blurred nationality, ethnicity and country boundaries. It has reaffirmed the reality of a global village, enabling teams to share information, to work together across borders and time zones. Distance is non-existent.

Created by Rick Smolan and Jennifer Erwitt, *24 Hours in Cyberspace: Painting on the Walls of the Digital Cave*, is a collection of photos and essays from around the world that beautifully captures the essence of our technological future.

One photo shows archaeologist, Scott Carroll sitting on the sand floor of a tent-like structure, surrounded by a Bedouin family, as he e-mails students around the world from the site of the ancient Coptic monastery about how the archaeological dig is progressing.

The Internet, while quietly carrying on for years, has become a raging world-wide phenomenon. So far its attraction has been its faithful bowing to the will of its users, reflecting their interests, concerns and demands in cyberspace. Regulatory forces however are attempting to define structure and parameters on this free communications forum. The outcome is yet undetermined, but be assured that the burgeoning Internet will be shaped, re-shaped and shaped yet again by changing needs, changing demands, changing challenges and changing opportunities.

One such "re-shaping" is already under way. U.S. universities that helped create the existing Internet are breaking away to establish Internet II since they have found the electronic traffic has become unbearable. Their new net will feature a wider bandwidth to increase speed tremendously.

Consider the impact today's technology has on your customers, on your business, on your strategic direction, on yourself.

The universe is full of magical things patiently waiting for our wits to grow sharper.

Eden Phillpots, Victorian writer

Consider the impact tomorrow's developing technology will have on your customers, on your business, on your strategic direction, on yourself. Consider your response, your action plan.

How technologically astute are you? Are you on the precipice of emerging technologies? What new opportunities can you create because of changing technology? What challenges can you address more efficiently because of changing technology? Develop a technology strategy that supports your business strategy.

When properly utilized, today's technology increases productivity. Recent business-oriented technologies such as fax, e-mail, Internet, Intranet, video conferencing, laptops with modems, have in many ways leveled the playing field for all businesses. Many smaller businesses look and act like big businesses. When size is factored out of the equation, "It's not the big that eat the small, it's the fast that eat the slow." Utilizing changing technology can make you one of "the fast."

Master change. Don't be mastered by it.

Sam Geist

Astute niche marketers have moved in to provide services once performed in-house by larger businesses. By forming strategic alliances with former competitors, they are able to re-new their marketplace position, demonstrating their own particular expertise. In our new world, they have successfully created opportunities, illustrating quite clearly why someone should do business with them.

KNOWLEDGE IS POWER

Distilled from data, extracted from information, knowledge rules. As today's most valuable currency, it is truly a king-maker. Technology opens new doors, knowledge holds them wide open. In developed countries the reliance on labor as the economic base is disappearing. Fortified by unprecedented technological advances, fueled by faster-than-instant communication, accelerated by free-market policies and aided by enlightened world trade policies, the information revolution is in full swing. The rewards go to the information keepers.

In the United States, exports of information technologies and related services now double that of aircraft, America's former top export.

Peter Drucker, expert management consultant, commented on the future of the industrialized world and our role in it, with his statement,

There will be no poor countries. There will only be ignorant countries.

Peter F. Drucker, management consultant and writer
U.S. News & World Report

"Manual labor, no matter how cheap, will not be able to compete with knowledge labor, no matter how well paid." The implication of this massive change in economic bases is staggering. It involves completely re-thinking the meaning of products so that information is included as a tangible *(and valuable)* resource. Supplying it effectively provides an internationally competitive advantage. Utilizing it effectively provides a local advantage.

Expand the value of the information you possess — by using it to enhance your company and its capability — by sharing it with your customers to increase their satisfaction. Add the power of your knowledge to the reasons that someone should do business with you, rather than someone else.

THE GLOBAL STRETCH

Spearheaded by the incessant need to find new markets and to satisfy emerging needs, marketers have sallied forth in search of global reach. The foreign office has become assimilated into an international landscape. The cry to be local and global simultaneously is clearly heard. The advantages of assuming this posture is recognized and applauded.

The "global stretch" concept presents tough challenges while offering great opportunities. It necessitates adopting a wider, future-focused perspective. It requires developing, re-developing and refining strategies. It demands incorporating a world-wide team approach where local offices demonstrate the best of their locality, yet meticulously exude a consistent global image.

When Domino's Pizza went global in the mid 1980s it took a one-pie-fits-all approach. It wasn't until the early 1990s, that it noticed that business, generally flat, was booming in a locally owned Japanese franchise that offered locally desired toppings. Domino's realized its one size approach was not in tune with its aspirations. By understanding local demands, like offering small individual pies in Germany and squid toppings in Japan, foreign sales skyrocketed.

Traditional, parochial perspectives no longer apply. The changes that must be made are not temporary, not transitory. They mirror systematic and permanent societal and workplace change. They demand an attitudinal shift. Question your niche, your position within a global perspective.

Do you fit in? Does your business fit in? How well? What can you change to ensure a better, tighter fit? How well have you shaken off the old mantle of price and quantity concerns and replaced them with value and service concerns?

> *[When conditions change] the same rules that worked so well in steadier times can misinform management and derail effective responses to new conditions. Unless the company is endowed with individuals who challenge old practices and, when necessary, violate company rules and policy — it won't be able to meet the difficult challenge of changing conditions.*
>
> Thomas V. Bonoma, Harvard Business School
> *Harvard Business Review*

...OR NOT

Remaining viable in today's marketplace requires forward movement. Maintaining a static position is in reality stepping backward. Today, no one can be anchored to what they did yesterday, no one can afford to watch and wait as competition *(local and now global)* passes them by.

The temptation is great to sit on the sidelines in the ostrich position. The fear of the unknown is not new. It has daunted us for centuries. Now is the perfect time to overcome this desire to hide — to use your own strength to embrace change to your own advantage.

Economists predict that nations (*read corporations, companies, entrepreneurs within those nations*) that try to resist change will simply find themselves left behind.

E. F. Borisch, Product Manager of the Milwaukee Gear Company expressed the inherent reluctance to change in his article in *Product Engineering* in 1959. He listed 50 reasons we/it/they can't change.

1. *We've never done it before.*
2. *Nobody else has ever done it.*
3. *It has never been tried before.*
4. *We tried it before.*
5. *Another company/person tried it before.*
6. *We've been doing it this way for 25 years.*
7. *It won't work in a small company.*
8. *It won't work in a large company.*
9. *It won't work in our company.*
10. *Why change — it's working OK.*
11. *The boss will never buy it.*
12. *It needs further investigation.*
13. *Our competitors are not doing it.*
14. *It's too much trouble to change.*
15. *Our company is different.*
16. *The ad department says it can't be done.*
17. *The sales department says it can't be done.*
18. *The service department won't like it.*
19. *The janitor says it can't be done.*
20. *It can't be done.*
21. *We don't have the money.*

22. We don't have the personnel.
23. We don't have the equipment.
24. The union will scream.
25. It's too visionary.
26. You can't teach an old dog new tricks.
27. It's too radical a change.
28. It's beyond my responsibility.
29. It's not my job.
30. We don't have the time.
31. It will obsolete other procedures.
32. Customers won't buy it.
33. It's contrary to policy.
34. It will increase overhead.
35. The employees will never buy it.
36. It's not our problem.
37. I don't like it.
38. You're right, but....
39. We're not ready for it.
40. It needs more thought.
41. Management won't accept it.
42. We can't take the chance.
43. We'd lose money on it.
44. It takes too long to pay out.
45. We're doing all right as it is.
46. It needs committee study.
47. Competition won't like it.
48. It needs sleeping on.
49. It won't work in this department.
50. It's impossible.

Little has changed.

Why this reluctance to make the change? We fear the process of re-education! Adults have invested endless hours of learning in growing accustomed to inches and miles; to February's 28 days; to "night" and "debt" with their silent letters; to qwertyuiop; and to all the rest. To introduce something altogether new would mean to begin all over, to become ignorant again, and to run the old, old risk of failing to learn.

Isaac Asimov, science writer and biochemist
Machines That Think

The last seven words of a dying business are "we've never done it that way before."

Which reasons have you used for why we/it/they can't change? Why? Ask yourself some pivotal questions. **What are you going to do in the face of this mammoth challenge? What is your plan? What innovative reasons can you offer to indicate "Why someone should do business with you...rather than someone else?"**

Whether we participate willingly or not, change affects us. By understanding the evolving world around us—by formulating responses that are appropriate for us today and relevant tomorrow—by remembering the last seven words of a dying business — and by being active, we can ride the crest of change, rather than drink the undertow.

Analyze, yes! Calculate, yes! Strategize, absolutely. But once all the deliberations and discussions and meetings are over—*act!*

Consider how you can adapt and incorporate the following 10 steps for changing times to your own situation in order to address your particular marketplace needs successfully.

TEN ACTION STEPS FOR CHANGING TIMES

1. Shift your perspective. Think differently.

FedEx thinks about delivery of products and information differently. It thinks how implementing new technology benefits its customers, and strengthens its marketplace position. Starbucks thinks about the pleasure of coffee differently. It thinks about its customers' need for enjoyment and relaxed diversion.

Think about today's needs. Think about tomorrow's needs.

Think innovatively.

2. Re-order your priorities.

Decide what is truly most important and do it first. One of Dr. Stephen Covey's 1996 *Highly Effective People Calendar* quotes states it simply: "The key is not to prioritize what's on your schedule, but to schedule your priorities." **Are your priorities in sync with your staff's, your customers', your suppliers' priorities?** Chemlawn *(a lawn maintenance company)* must have decided that outstanding customer service was its top priority, since service is exuded at every point of communication from the moment the operator picks up the telephone, until after the grass is sprayed. It leaves its customers knowing that they are Chemlawn's top priority.

> *In the new information society, where the only constant is change, we can no longer expect to get an education and be done with it. There is no one education, no one skill that lasts a lifetime now. Like it or not, the information society has turned us all into lifetime learners.*
>
> John Naisbitt, business writer and researcher
> *Megatrends*

3. Develop faster reflexes.

Fence-sitting is out. Decision making and a call to action are in. The Internet's ability to link thousands of computer networks has opened untold opportunities for future-focused organizations. They see the Internet as dramatically increasing their communicability, from sending e-mail messages around the world to surfing the World Wide Web in search of almost anything *(information or product or service)* imaginable. Involvement continues to grow exponentially since many companies have taken the no-time-to-lose attitude and jumped aboard to broaden their market exposure.

4. Get focused. Stay focused.

Find out what's really important *(to you and your customers)*. Find out what works and concentrate on that. Wal-Mart focuses on low prices every day, because that's what its customers want. It works. It has built an empire on it.

5. Simplify.

Search for easier solutions. A better approach. The St. Lawrence Centre, a large theater in Toronto offers its subscribers quick, no hassle ticket exchange by phone. It has made it easy, a benefit of membership. All Nations Furniture Assemblers is one of a growing number of companies across North America that offers its customers the service of having their newly purchased ready-to-assemble furniture professionally assembled within hours of delivery. It fulfills a need! Makes it simple!!

6. Be flexible.

Think of your options as a tool chest full of tools. Choose the most appropriate tool to meet the challenge — not the one you always use. By using new techniques, by altering your thinking patterns, by taking advantage of available, even untried resources, your response will be all the more on the mark. Many service stations today exhibit a flexible service approach, offering both self-service and full service, pay at the pump, or pay the attendant. Gas only or sundries too. Fast food kiosks, bonuses, gifts, smiles. Stations recognize marketplace challenges and are innovatively trying to meet them.

7. Overcome the fear of flying.

The fear of failure, of heights, of flying. Fear inhibits the ability to change on a personal and on a business level. Work at conquering it. *"Will it work? Will they like it? What if?"* debilitates and stagnates. Remember that very old, but relevant maxim, *(slightly altered), "To try and have failed is infinitely more productive than never to have tried at all."* Tim Hortons, a coffee and donut chain which originated in Canada, realized that donuts and muffins and coffee weren't enough anymore. It agonized over introducing new products. Would customers like its new product line?

Its bagels are a big hit — proving it is decidedly better to have tried and....

You miss 100 percent of the shots you never take.

Wayne Gretzky,
NHL hockey player

8. Become a problem solver.

Customers want solutions. Think of all the solutions, so many of them simple to provide, that customers have been delighted to incorporate into their lives: answering machines, portable phones, highlighters, Post-it Notes, low/no fat, e-mail, next-to-instant delivery. Cheaper, faster, more convenient instabanking. **What problems can you solve? What solutions can you offer?**

9. Energize.

Remember the commercial for the Energizer battery? It just keeps going and going and going. An "energizer" builds momentum, creates a company culture that is action-oriented, future-focused and keeps the organization moving. Terry Fox, Canada's one-legged runner, mobilized an entire country with his energy, his commitment and his undaunting spirit to fight cancer. He left a legacy that continues to keep his goals alive and moving.

10. Listen.

Although the winds of change may howl loudly, the opportunities they carry sometimes whisper very softly. Finely segmented markets spring up in the unlikeliest places. Recognize them. Create them. Micro-breweries, furniture assembly, exotic ethnic foods, new magazines, new categories of cookbooks, old movie fans, and on and on. Develop your own niche market.

All indications are that our future will be more change filled than ever before. As the rate of change continues to accelerate, our response must match its velocity to remain in sync. Move forward or....

"Why should someone do business with you...rather than someone else?"

ASK. ANSWER. PLAN. CHANGE.

There is no "finished."

Sam Geist

Ask yourself these critical questions on change. Find and incorporate action-oriented answers into your everyday business experience.

1. Why should someone do business with you...rather than someone else? Why should someone do business with you *tomorrow*...rather than someone else?

_____

_____

_____

_____

_____

_____

2. How informed are you about the changing marketplace, about emerging technologies?

_____

_____

_____

_____

_____

3. What are you doing to increase your knowledge, your information about the changing marketplace, about emerging technologies?

_____

_____

_____

_____

_____

4. What are you changing in your organization as a result of newfound information to stay on the cutting edge of change?

_____

_____

_____

_____

5. How are you positioning your organization to take advantage of technological advances and emerging technologies? Are you taking tomorrow into account in your positioning decisions?

_____

_____

_____

_____

_____

6. What new *(within the last year)* advantages are you providing your customers that you did not previously provide? What new advantages are you planning for next year?

_____

_____

_____

_____

_____

7. What specific trends significantly affect your customers? What are you and your organization doing for your customers that is in sync with these trends?

_____

_____

_____

_____

_____

8. What do you provide your staff to learn about the emerging marketplace, about change? How do you enable them to act on this information?

_____

_____

_____

_____

_____

9. How do you communicate your goals about change to your staff? What are you doing to ensure they understand, inculcate and effectively incorporate these goals into their work environment?

_____

_____

_____

_____

10. How are you using today's marketplace trends to attract new customers?

_____

_____

_____

_____

11. How are you encouraging existing customers to buy more, more often or use more of your services, more often?

_____

_____

_____

_____

12. How many different solutions to a problem are you able to provide your customers?

_____

_____

_____

_____

13. What are your top five excuses for not changing?

_____

_____

_____

_____

14. What can you do to eliminate these five excuses?

_____

_____

_____

_____

15. What are your top priorities? How are they in sync with today's marketplace? With today's customers? Do these priorities have a window of opportunity into tomorrow?

_____

_____

_____

_____

_____

16. From how many different perspectives do you view the changing marketplace? List them.

_____

_____

_____

_____

17. How fast do you respond to change? What can you do to speed up your reaction time?

_____

_____

_____

_____

18. What are you doing to simplify your customers' experiences with you, with your organization?

_____

_____

_____

_____

19. What do you do in your role as the organization's energizer to keep your organization moving?

_____

_____

_____

_____

20. When was the last time you asked your customers why they do business with you? With your competitors? What did you discover?

_____

_____

_____

_____

21. **When was the last time you asked your former customers why they stopped doing business with you? What was their response?**

_____

_____

_____

_____

Write in one additional question you feel is important to you, your situation as a result of reading this section — *and then answer it.*

Q. _____

_____

_____

_____

_____

_____

A. _____

_____

_____

_____

_____

_____

Part two focuses on relationships — on building them, maintaining them and growing them. Who you are and where you and your organization are headed, are examined from your customers' point of view. Pertinent questions are asked throughout to assist you to get closer to your customers — and answer *"Why should someone do business with you...rather than someone else?"* A demographic outline of target markets is included as an addendum to this section.

A Business Without Customers...Isn't

2

How do you get and keep your customers?

You have to know your customers: who they are, what they want and need and what they are willing to pay for. You must see eye-to-eye with them and regard the marketplace from their viewpoint. **Do you?**

Relationships are initiated by similarities and built on common interest. They are sustained by shared benefit, by the what's-in-it-for-me factor.

Why should someone do business with you...rather than someone else?

Find the answers from your customers' perspective to "What's in it for me."

Determine:

- *what you and your organization are all about*

- *where you are headed*

- *who your customers are right now, who they will be tomorrow*

- *what your customers want now, what they will want tomorrow*

> **It is hard to solve a problem when you don't even know it exists.**
>
> Fred Heiser, Chairman
> Heiser-Egan, Inc.

WHO ARE YOU?

Take a good, long objective look at who you are. **What do you see at the heart and soul of your organization? Where are you focusing your energies? Do your customers know who you are? Who you want to be? Do they care?**

WHERE ARE YOU HEADED?

Everyone in the marketplace moves somewhere. Some slowly, some slower. Even standing still is moving — *backward!*

Where are you going? What do you see? Have you caught a glimpse of your customers en route? Spoken to them, initiated a dialogue or are you mumbling to yourself?

Are you satisfied with your anticipated destination? If you aren't, put into motion the mechanics to change. It requires action rather than discussion. Develop focus, initiate objectives and vision-ize toward goals.

> *If managers are careless about basic things — telling the truth, respecting moral codes, proper professional conduct — who can believe them on other issues?*
>
> James L. Hayes, President
> American Management Association
> *Memos for Management: Leadership*

Focus on the most important element in your business: your customers. After all *a business without customers...isn't.*

Share *your* vision, *your* goals. Sharing doesn't take root overnight. Sharing grows out of changing policy, changing operations, changing attitude, changing empowerment on a corporate level. It culminates in changing accountability, moving from a "that's-not-my-problem, not-my-department" approach to one actively seeking customer oriented solutions.

Realization quietly dawns that everything begins and ends with customers—that your customers' perception is the real world. Recognizing and satisfying customers' needs, expectations, demands, becomes the modus operandi.

The death knell for that atrophying refrain, *"but we've always done it that way"* finally sounds. Information is sought. Assumptions are questioned. Decisions become fact based, rather than tradition based.

My focus is not on selling. It's more on making sure that people who become clients are willing and able to pay for my services. Then I concentrate on providing service—I simply help clients buy what they need. I'm always in a problem-solving mode, and that puts me on the client's side of the table.

Don Ray, financial planner and management consultant, FSC Securities Corporation *Financial Strategies*

Individual departments lose their exclusive, autonomous status to become part of the whole organization, benefiting everyone. A new responsible demeanor develops. "Doing it right the first time" becomes more important than "let's get together and solve this crisis." You'll notice the change, so will your customers.

A personal experience I had not long ago hit home the value of instilling a responsible customer-focused attitude throughout an organization from top to bottom.

My car was at a local GM dealer for repairs *again*, repairs that had not been completed satisfactorily the first time. When I went into the garage to pick up my car, the work order was still taped to

Set and demand standards of excellence. Anybody who accepts mediocrity—in school, in job, in life—is a guy who compromises. And when the leader compromises, the whole damn organization compromises.

Charles Knight Emerson
Speaker's Library of Business Stories, Anecdotes & Humor, Joe Griffith

my side window. Climbing in, I reached over to tear it off.

Its format caught my eye. A blank area occupied the top half of the form. It is here the mechanic fills in the reason service was requested. The bottom half of the form contained two boxes, with information for the garage beside each. It is the mechanic's responsibility to check off one of the boxes. The box indicating "second visit, same repair" had been checked off on my form. I was amazed. I was angry. When management accepts, even expects that so many of the repairs completed will necessitate "bring-it-in-again" service, that they incorporate this eventuality on the form, how can anything else result? Frontline staff merely reflect the nonchalant attitude demonstrated by management.

Efficiency is doing the thing right. Effectiveness is doing the right thing.

Peter F. Drucker,
management consultant and writer
Profit

Focusing on customers' needs, on customers' perspectives often requires a relationship re-alignment. The newly developed relationship must satisfactorily answer for each partner, *what's in it for me?* It must operate on the assumption that the unique needs, demands and expectations of each customer are understood and satisfied, that both you and your customers are headed in the same direction.

Customers expect it!

Ed Mirvish of Toronto, famous for his Honest Ed's discount store, built an empire on understanding and satisfying this supposition. With his well known penchant for simplicity, he reveals his secret strategy:

- *Satisfy a need!*

- *Go against the trend!*

- *Keep it simple!*

He has used this strategy successfully to satisfy his customers' needs for decades. And they keep coming back for more. He is remembered for his zany antics and wild marketing schemes, but more than that, he is remembered and respected for his vision and his understanding of human nature. He is there because his customers are still there.

> *Thinking like your customers think today, isn't enough. You must think like your customers will think tomorrow. Anticipate their needs and expectations.*
>
> Sam Geist

Planning a Body Shop makeover for U.S. locations, Steen Kanter, CEO (U.S.) understands the necessity of satisfying customers to stay ahead. "We want to and must become a retailer and start thinking and looking through the customer's eyes."

Successful marketers concentrate on where they are going. And where they're going is where their customers are going. They realize they can't be everything to everyone. Focusing everywhere at once dilutes the intensity of their effort. They choose as their primary thrust the area of greatest strength and greatest possibility: the unique value they can deliver — the special extras their customers want. They work at becoming so powerful, so absolutely invincible in their niche that competitors can't come close.

What is your most powerful weapon? In what areas are you head and shoulders above your competition?

Choose your unique value, your special attribute, the one that is:

- *most important to your customers*

- *the area where you can satisfy them best*
  and then use it. Become a force to be reckoned with.

Follow in the steps of success. There is much to learn from others. Successful companies realize in order to get where they want to go, they have to provide something of unique value that is important to their customers, and do it better than their competitors.

Sam's Warehouse Club, the powerful chain created by Sam Walton, and Price Club/Costco, don't try to be all things to all people. They don't have boutique pretensions. They don't search out small, exclusive niche markets. They don't provide a lot of customer service. They don't feature aesthetically exciting fixtures or displays.

Create The Perfect Fit.

Sam Geist

They focus on providing selected mass-market products, conveniently, at the best price. They have determined that's what their customers want: mainstream products, priced better than anyone else and a no-hassle, easy-to-participate shopping experience. They concentrate their considerable energies to satisfying these customer demands.

Sam's Warehouse Club and Price Club/Costco focus on execution excellence. They standardize, simplify and tightly control every aspect of their businesses to optimize processes, minimize costs and hassles, maximize efficiencies.

They utilize the latest technological tools to assist them to communicate, to move merchandise, to eliminate waste, to bump up profitability. They run tight ships. They maintain their focus at all costs to make good on their promise to their customers — to be *the* low cost operators. Their customers believe them and so they return to their stores, bringing friends with them.

Starbucks, the coffee emporium based in Seattle doesn't try to be all things to all people. It doesn't shout fast food. It concentrates on what it knows its customers want: the experience of coffee in a sleek nouveau environment, a hot sip of luxury, a small slice of gratification. Starbucks out-of-the-box thinking has updated those warmly remembered coffee houses of the 1960s, with a sophisticated gloss demanded by today's Boomers. It has established niche dominance by understanding the market it services. It realizes its enviable position is dependent on challenging its own parameters — striving for renewal — re-inventing itself again and again to separate itself from its competitors.

It focuses on flavor, on quality, on creative and delicious products. It focuses on being at the top of tomorrow. Its customers are looking for a little indulgence, sophisticated surroundings, an opportunity to meet and greet, a chance to be the first to try the newest. Starbucks provides it. The latest blends. The freshest beans. The most au courant drinks. The most indulgent treats. Customers love it. They drink. They eat. They smile. They carry home little Starbucks bags of Starbucks beans and they return, bringing their friends with them.

> *To win through customer intimacy, "the product is conceived at the customer's office."*
>
> Gabriel Battista, President & CEO
> Cable & Wireless
> *Fortune*

Lands' End, catalog for yuppie, sporty America, doesn't try to be all things to all people. It doesn't look to be cheapest. It concentrates on what it knows *its customers* want: well-tailored quality.

To know which well-tailored quality fashion to feature in its catalog, Lands' End focuses on knowing—*really knowing* its customers. It conducts research to glean a high level of customer information. It knows its customers like family so it is able to communicate to a market of one. It establishes and maintains high percentages of repeat business with high levels of customer satisfaction by constantly striving to upgrade its offerings. Its objective is to stay ahead of its customers' rising expectations.

Lands' End focuses on tightening customer bonds. It focuses on strengthening customer loyalty, on providing the very solutions to problems that its customers want. It makes its customers' lives easier, so they order, and order again. Customers tell their friends so they too become part of the Lands' End family.

The Home Depot, the do-it-yourself home improvement giant, has attained an enviable level of excellence in the do-it-yourself market. It concentrates on what it knows *its customers* want: complete selection and professional advice.

Customers control profitability. A five percent increase in customer retention equals between 25 percent and 80 percent increase in profit.

Harvard Business School Study

There was a time when the local hardware store offered knowledgeable advice. As home improvement stores grew to football field size, service disappeared. The Home Depot has changed the complexion of the industry with its experienced staff. It focuses on the nuts and bolts of do-it-yourself: *information.* It focuses on the details of the project, — all the components to complete the job. It realizes that sustaining its niche is dependent on maintaining its staff advantage. At The Home Depot, frontline truly is bottomline. Its customers trust it and appreciate its advice. They buy, complete their projects and then buy again to begin new projects. Their friends see the results of those visits to The Home Depot and they too become customers.

Many companies and organizations try to be all things to all people. Some, because they work hard at it, improve. Some become successful because they maintain continual commitment to their customers. However where the "I do it all!" organizations fail is in their ability to reach new standards of excellence, achieve new heights in outstanding performance.

We will either find a way or make one.

Hannibal, (247-183 B.C.)
Carthaginian General who crossed the Alps to fight Rome

They aren't able to create a breakthrough in any one focus because they try to cover so many.

Know what your customers care about, and work toward providing that unique value which makes you outstanding.

WHO ARE YOUR CUSTOMERS?

Find out who your best customers are. Find out everything you can about them. Buying habits — buying decisions *(whether at the retail level, service level or professional level)* are very clearly reflected in the wide diversity of today's lifestyles. Take a glimpse at the many niche markets that have sprung up and the bevy of targeted services that have emerged to address them as an indication of the magnitude of diversity.

With the growing number of two-income families employing the services of nannies for their infants and small children, it wasn't a total surprise to hear about "nanny cams" — a hidden wide-angle camera, that monitors in-home caregivers. Hundreds of firms specializing in surveillance equipment have sprung up in the last few years, since many Boomer parents want to ensure their new nanny is providing conscientious, high-quality child care.

Consumers are statistics,
customers are people.

Stanley Marcus, Chairman emeritus
Neiman-Marcus
A Passion for Excellence, Peters & Austin

Create your own opportunities by tuning in very closely to your target market or to the markets you want to reach. Learn about their backgrounds, their motivations, needs and tastes. Determine how you can satisfy them more advantageously than everyone else. Determine how you can add value differently than everyone else.

Who are your best customers? Do you really know them?

Build your business around your *best customers*. Know your target markets from a demographic perspective — their ages, their lifestyles, their household formation. Know your target market from a needs/wants point of view. Know your target market from life situations, from gender, from ethnicity. Find out how to reach them, how to satisfy them. Know them on a one-to-one basis. Recognize that your best customers belong to more than just one group *(since niche markets abound)*. Recognize that your customers first and foremost are individuals.

To become more familiar with the characteristics of your target markets, their wants and needs, a demographic addendum to part two (beginning on page 52) has been included. It outlines segments of the North American marketplace according to the criteria just mentioned. By understanding what motivates your customers, by realizing what is important in their lives, you are better able to provide it, whether it be needed services or desired merchandise.

Although statistics don't provide a personal profile, they do provide a starting point for relationship building. Much demographic and statistical information is available in both Canada and the United States and is a valuable addition to your existing arsenal of customer knowledge.

Learn about your customers today, learn about the marketplace

We tend to view everyone as part of a mass market. But there are no mass answers today. If you take 100 people who have one foot on a block of ice and the other foot in a fireplace you can argue that the average person is comfortable. In reality, no one's average. Look for individual solutions rather than mass solutions.

Watts Wacker, Yankelovich Partners Inc.

for those you would like as customers, look into the future and try to determine who your customers will be as we move into the next millennium.

Ask yourself these questions to ensure you really know your best customers.

1. **How large is the target group's market size?**

2. **To what household group do they belong?**

3. **What is their income level? Does this income level enable discretionary purchasing?**

4. **To what age group do they belong?**

5. **To what ethnic group do they belong? To what "life circumstances" group do they belong? (eg. disabled)**

6. **What cultural traditions and customs are important to them?**

7. **Who influences your target market?**

8. **In what life stage do they find themselves?**

9. **What do they value foremost: convenience? price? service? quality?**

10. **What do they read? How do they spend their leisure time?**

The answers to these questions will assist you to focus beneficially on your target market. They will give you the opportunity to educate yourself about your customers. They will demonstrate quite clearly how customers *(and their lives)* are changing. As a marketer you must change along with them.

> *Remember your customers are changing — don't assume you can pigeonhole them for the long term based on what they want, buy or tell you today.*
>
> Sam Geist

Develop techniques for getting close to your customers. They will highlight the means to enlarge your market.

AN ASIDE

Always look to broadening your market. It is a lifeline to survival.

I heard an interesting statistic that clearly illustrates the advantages of subscribing to this approach at a National Grocery Conference I participated in. Grocery store customers who buy diapers spend 2 1/2 times as much in the store as those who don't buy diapers — to the tune of $70 per weekly shopping trip. Why? Quite simply because their needs run to baby foods, baby supplies, in addition to diapers. This stage in family life also precludes more eating in than at later family life stages.

When you want customers to do business with you rather than someone else, you must give them "the why." Know yourself better, know where you and your organization are heading, know where your customers are and know what they want.

Newsweek magazine, recognized the importance of delivering a personalized approach when they decided to feature as the lead story in their December 1992 issue, the social and psychological significance of Boomers turning 50. At newsstands everywhere, *Newsweek's* "Woman Turning 50" cover was displayed next to *Newsweek's* "Man Turning 50" cover. The articles inside both magazines were identical, but the covers heightened identification with readers' concerns by targeting to each gender so specifically.

> *The customer is the judge, jury and executioner.*
>
> Sam Geist

Marketers asking and answering the question, ***"Why should someone do business with you...rather than someone else?"*** must always keep at the forefront of their thoughts, their plans, their actions, that overwhelmingly popular world-wide reaching radio station WIFM, *(what's-in-it-for-me)*. It is your responsibility to provide viable solutions that meet *(or better yet)* exceed your market's expectations.

Why should someone do business with you...rather than someone else?"

ASK. ANSWER. PLAN. CHANGE.

These 21 questions will help you focus on the task at hand: getting and keeping customers — the reason you are in business. Ask and answer them by yourself — for yourself.

1. Why should someone do business with you...rather than someone else?

_____

_____

_____

_____

2. What makes you and your organization "tick?"

_____

_____

_____

_____

3. In our ever-moving marketplace, where are you headed?

_____

_____

_____

_____

4. Are your customers aware of who you are and where you are going?

_____

_____

_____

_____

5. What do your customers really want from you? What do they really expect?

_____

_____

_____

_____

6. Do you know which of their needs and expectations matter most to them? List them.

_____

_____

_____

_____

7. Are you able to meet those wants and expectations right now at a cost they are willing to pay for? How well?

_____

_____

_____

_____

8. Customers' needs change. Will you be able to meet their wants and expectations in five years? How well?

_____

_____

_____

_____

9. How well is your competition meeting customers' wants and expectations? Are they succeeding better than you? What can you adapt from their success?

_____

_____

_____

_____

10. What can you do to go beyond just satisfying, to truly delighting your customers? Are you doing it today?

_____

_____

_____

_____

11. Who is your primary target market? What other target markets are important to you?

_____

_____

_____

_____

12. What research have you done to ensure you have accurately determined your target markets? What feedback have you received?

_____

_____

_____

_____

13. What are you doing now to ensure an ongoing dialogue with your target market? Is it successful? How do you know?

_____

_____

_____

_____

14. What strategies can you incorporate into your business plan to enlarge your target markets?

_____

_____

_____

15. Does your business focus lie with a people perspective or a product/service perspective? How long ago was your focus established?

_____

_____

_____

_____

16. Is your focus still appropriate? Does it need updating, revising? What can you do to update, revise your focus? Are you?

_____

_____

_____

_____

_____

_____

17. What is the potential "lifetime value" of your primary target market?

_____

_____

_____

_____

_____

_____

18. What are you doing to realize and enhance this potential value?

_____

_____

_____

_____

_____

_____

19. What one single thing can you do tomorrow to convert a consumer into your customer? Will you? What one thing can you do tomorrow to convert a casual customer to a loyal customer? Will you?

20. If your organization disappeared today, would it be missed? Why?

21. If you were starting your business today, what would you do differently?

Write in one additional question you feel is important to you, your situation as a result of reading this section — *and then answer it.*

Q. _____

_____

_____

_____

_____

_____

_____

_____

_____

A. _____

_____

_____

_____

_____

_____

_____

_____

_____

TARGET MARKETS ADDENDUM

Target market statistics are readily available. Information, categorized by household, age, ethnicity, income and lifestyle abounds. This marketplace data has been included to assist you get a sense of North American consumers. While it identifies major consumer groups according to their attributes, wants/needs and offers information to reach and satisfy them, it is not intended as a complete, in-depth analysis and should not be construed as such. Information was determined to be accurate at time of printing.

To compile the information with relevance for both the American and Canadian marketplace, the following sources were used: *Canadian Social Trends, Statistics Canada, American Demographics and Consumer Trends, The Toronto Star, USA Today, The Wall Street Journal and Sampling, Modelling and Research Technologies*, a marketing research firm. Much of the information is applicable to both the United States and Canada. When information is specific to only one country, it is so indicated.

In reality, knowing your customers requires more than data mastery, however the more you know about your customers the better you are able to connect, to serve and to hold them. Unless you understand your customers and their unique situations and feelings, you won't know how to best advise and sell them what they want and what they need.

When your own tooth aches, you know how to sympathize with one who has a toothache.

Chinese proverb

As you read through these target market designations, determine where your customers fit in, how they are affected by their marketplace position, and how they themselves influence the marketplace. Keep in mind that every customer belongs to several groups at the same time.

Target your products, your services, your value-added benefits to your market(s) effectively by considering their unique characteristics, problems, needs and interests.

Framing all target market designations is household formation. Sociologists have long recognized the importance of the family group. It affects needs, interests, challenges, desires and spending habits of its members. Clearly, the needs and purchasing patterns of a single mother with small children is vastly different from those of an "empty nester."

Only by identifying the family group to which your customers belong can you hope to begin to provide viable solutions. Household dynamics must be factored into your marketing and communications equation. Questions such as **Where is your customer's household today? Where will it be in 15 years?** must be answered. Take note of growing segments. Their increase has appreciable consequences. Anticipate lifestyle changes as groups age. This dramatically affects purchasing. **How can you capitalize on this statistical information? What are the implications for your organization?**

Are you aware?

- In the United States more than 60 percent of African American households with children were headed by a single mother in 1994. In many inner cities the figure exceeded 80 percent.

- In 1991, 20 percent of Canadian households with children were one-parent households. In the United States the figure was found to be 25 percent.

- In Canada, 50 percent of family households consist of mother, father and children.

- Diversification into increasingly smaller and non-family households continues to increase.

- Marriage is becoming less central to family life, however children and other relatives are becoming increasingly important to the family unit.

- Family members *(including grown and absent children)* continue to provide a major focus of social life and support.

- Family influences are still important in purchasing decisions.

- Emotional bonds and interpersonal influences are as strong as ever.

- Parental influence can encourage or discourage purchasing decision of children.

TARGET MARKETS BY AGE

Age is an influential target market determinator. Marketers and analysts alike have divided our marketplace into four main age groups:

- youth (babies, kids, teens)

- the X-generation (20s - early 30s)

- the Baby Boomers (early 30s - 50s)

- graying population (50+)

[Note: There are also sub-groups within each age group, for example the Junior Seniors (50 to 64 years), Middle Seniors (65 to 74 years) and the Senior Seniors (75 years and older)].

YOUTH

Who are they?

- babies

- kids

- teens

In the last decade, children's economic power has grown faster than any other age group.

How do you reach and satisfy them?

- recognize that they are both purchasers and influencers of

What do they want/need?

- *"cool" brand names to match their image and personal needs*

- *sustenance, nurturing*

- *"what everyone else has" in order to belong to their peer group*

- *fun*

purchases *(by parents, grandparents, peers)*

- group *(kids, teens)* is very media *(TV, radio, Internet)* sensitive

- group *(teens)* is peer influenced by word of mouth

- concentrate on *(teens)* their leaders and influencers

- enhance their ability to be part of the group

- develop opportunities for their parents/grandparents to feel they are fulfilling their responsibilities in the care and feeding of their young.

Are you aware?

- This group is a technologically literate group, growing up at the computer keyboard. They are willing to embrace virtual reality. Ready customers for computers, the Internet and its shopping, educational and communication opportunities. Canadian research of "screen-agers" *(i.e. nine-to-14-year old "tweens")* reported in *The Toronto Star,* (November 1996) indicates an explosion of computer use, especially in high-income families *(earning about $70,000+ a year).*

  - 60 percent of "tweens" *(nine-to-14 years)* now have computers at home *(up 90 percent from one year ago)*

  - 39 percent have Internet access at school *(up 15 percent from one year ago)*

- Loyal to brands that help them look good. Boomers, with their penchant to buy the best for their babies and their toddlers have fostered and supported an entire industry of designer children's clothes and educational toys.

- Boomers want their children to reflect their own sense of style and their own academic brilliance.

- The best-fed ever. The connection of good food with good brains was confirmed long ago. It is therefore assumed that better food results in better brains, hence the phenomenal growth of gourmet, "premium" baby food in the United States. Earth's Best Inc., the biggest independent producer of organic baby foods, continues to expand, based on its customers' belief that its products are best for baby.

- Teens wield tremendous buying power, because almost all their earnings consist of disposable income, designated for clothes, entertainment, food and fun. In 1994, American teens had an aggregate income of $96 billion.

- Teens' purchases reflect what they think of themselves and how they wish to be perceived. Purchasing is made as an act of independence, conformity, self-expression, and socialization.

- Statistics in *American Demographics and Consumer Trends* indicate that each year children spend more than $14.4

billion of their own money, and influence $132 billion in adults' spending. Kids allowances alone reach $20 billion.

■ Boys spend more of their own money than girls. Girls spend more of family's money.

■ Almost one-third of U.S. 18-and 19-year-olds hold a credit card in their name.

■ Today's two career North American households have created a generation of independent children with unprecedented influence over all sorts of family purchasing. They assume more responsibility for household shopping than did children of this age group previously because both parents work.

■ Statistics indicate that children in one-parent households become independent shoppers at an even earlier age than children from two parent families.

■ Older teens feel the teen label refers to someone much younger than themselves and therefore don't like it.

■ Retailers can boost sales by making their environment kid-friendly — designed so child can be occupied while adult shops.

I spend about $50 a week, mostly on food and incidentals, when I go shopping for clothes, I spend a lot more.

Allan Denton, age 17
(in an interview)

GENERATION XERS

Who are they?

- represent 50 million North Americans born from 1965-1974*

- market power of $200 billion a year

- their lifestyle strongly affects their spending habits — many leave home and marry later than this age group has done in any previous generation

- have higher college attendance, but graduation rates are not higher than previous generation of graduates and their income is lower

- insecurity and slow transition to adulthood characterize their lives

- a group as diverse as the coffee shops, malls, college campuses, subway stations and sporting events that are their popular hangouts

What do they want/need?

- *simple, straightforward communication*
- *lack of hype*
- *a little understanding, a lot of respect*
- *large ticket items such as cars, electronic & computer equipment, fitness & athletic equipment, clothing and travel*

Note: David Foot co-author of Boom, Bust & Echo, a demographic look at Canada, defines Generation X as born between 1960 and 1966, with the Baby Bust generation born between 1967 and 1979 following them. However, American demographers in general use the criteria outlined here.

How do you reach and satisfy them?

- on electronic media

- by honest, direct approach

- with small well-targeted bites *(or bytes)* of information

- provide honest solutions

- provide products and services that appeal to their lifestyle, and fulfill their genuine needs rather than targeting toward status orientation

Are you aware?

- Their purchasing priorities change along with changes in their concerns. Instead of buying "stuff" they are beginning to buy financial security with mutual funds and other investments.

- Xers understand the critical importance of education, yet are frustrated with their inability to achieve the schooling they would like. They therefore become an eager market for adult education and job-related training.

- Seek a balance between work and leisure. Not as driven as Boomers. Not willing to sacrifice personal lives for grand achievement.

- Remain at home much longer than previous groups their age. Fifty percent continue to live at home through their late 20s. Many are part of a "boomerang" family, having left and returned home.

- Have become the designated decision

The media always focus on extremes, and they're too quick to label people. I slacked for a few months, but then I got on with my life. Today, most of my friends my age are working hard. We don't have a vision of a goal for our careers yet, like our parents did.

Terry Neeson, age 29
(in an interview)

makers for parents and other relatives in their area of expertise: electronic entertainment equipment, computers, automobiles, etc.

- Purchasers of product and services that allow them to stay in touch and in control (fax machines, cell phones, beepers).

- Dedicated users of the Internet.

- Search out products and services that fulfill a genuine need.

BABY BOOMERS

Who are they?

- born between 1946 and 1965/66

- oldest turned 50 in 1995/96

- represent a 78 million bulge in population in the United States and 9.8 million in Canada

- huge buying and trend setting power because of their huge numbers *(almost 33 percent of the Canadian population and 31 percent of the U.S. population)*

- most affluent of all groups *(oldest of the Boomers)*

- biggest spenders *(oldest of the Boomers)*

What do they want/need?
- *save time*
- *stay young*
- *keep fit*
- *convenience*
- *maintain their strong sense of individualism*
- *"to get away"*
- *find relief from the responsibilities to parents and children*

How do you reach and satisfy them?

- address their needs, fears

- build rapport with them by mirroring their attitudes and lifestyle. Be aware not to lump them together with mature market as they hit 50+. They don't want to be regarded like their parents.

- provide customer service and product knowledge

- provide convenience through delivery, assembly, installation

- deliver "value"

- deliver on needs and expectations

- provide "fun," a good time. Create a pleasurable experience.

- offer customization, immediacy, value
  (must know customer extremely well to do this)

Are you aware?

- Huge blips of interest emerge and change as the Boomers age, representing their changing needs, wants and interests. For example, the enormous interest in tennis and jogging a few years ago is giving way to an increased interest in golf as Boomers' activities now accommodate their *(spoken in a whisper)* aging bodies.

- At-home interests are being translated into a tremendous increase in gardening activities. Gardening related sales, plants, books, equipment are reaching all-time highs.

- Cooking has become their latest hobby. The answer to "what's for dinner?" is not reservations as frequently as it was. Along with this interest in cooking, there is a rise in demand for new foods, grains such as couscous, fresh herbs and seasonings, flavored oils & vinegars, new rices and so on. U.S.-based Williams-Sonoma is currently being followed by a host of other stores for today's serious cooks, catering to Boomers in the kitchen with the quality kitchenware they demand. Why the increase in pleasure/leisure cooking? It's done by choice. It's now "want to" rather than "have to."

- Precious "relaxing at home" time is often used to read for information, for pleasure, for do-it-yourself. Chapters, Barnes & Noble, Borders — mega-book stores — cater to this market's renewed interest in reading by providing out-standing selection.

- "Do-it-Yourself" claims a sizable portion of Boomers leisure time. Their interest has spawned numerous TV how-to shows, hundreds of books *(more books start with how-to than any other category)* and tapes, and of course, the sprouting of a handyman's dream — The Home Depot.

- Although Boomers' activities reflect their aging, they will nevertheless be the most active 50-year-olds ever. The last thing they want is to become like their parents. They still exercise religiously at the club or at home, utilizing an ever-growing variety of body enhancing equipment.

- Record number of Boomers are becoming Harley-Davidson bikers. The average age of a Harley rider is now 42 years. Ten years ago it was 34. Accountants, doctors and engineers dressed in their Harley tees are taking to the road to escape their office constraints. The demand for the Harley experience is so huge that dealers are sold out of new models a year in advance.

- Huge purchasers of anti-aging remedies, from creams to baldness cures, thereby encouraging further research.

- Huge purchasers of mutual funds.

- Act as free agents. Put personal needs ahead of group's.

- Independent thinkers. Don't follow fashion trends if it doesn't suit their needs. Remember the miniskirt disaster of the early 1990s when Boomer women refused to buy?

GRAYING POPULATION

Who are they?

- the mature market, 50+, 55+ or 65+
  (depending on the research group defining them)

- not a single market at all, but a diverse population that accounts for 43 percent of all U.S. households *(for 50+)*

- 85 years and over have become the United States' fastest growing age group. These "oldest-old" comprise 3.4 million Americans.

How do you reach and satisfy them?

- information, recommendations

- convenience, ease of doing business

- slower, leisurely pace for interaction

- build trust

- communicate appropriately to its wide diversity and wide age range

- market to these five values that are the root motivators of this group

  - autonomy, self-sufficiency

  - altruism

  - social correctness, spiritual correctness

  - personal growth

  - revitalization

- market to their thinking style *(a subjective, rather than objective one)*

- take capabilities and limitations into account

Are you aware?

- Snaps and closures on senior clothes are currently designed to be fastened by a spouse. And if there is no spouse...?

- "Fine viewer," a view finder by Boston Retail Products enlarges type on labels by 300 percent and is being used in pharmacies and supermarkets.

What do they want/need?

- *comfortable clothes, easy-to-dress-alone wear*
- *comfortable, safe shopping environment, with non-slip floors, easy-to-see-and-reach merchandise*
- *fashionability, stylish clothes, attractively displayed*
- *people contact — relationships, interaction*
- *service*

- Studies indicate that seniors, because of their stability *(they are much less likely to move)* and their loyalty, actually remain customers longer than younger customers.

- "Woopies" *(Well Off Older People)* are big computer consumers because they have the time and money. SeniorsNet, a World Wide Web site is one of many that targets to the over-50 market.

- Purchase 25 percent of all toys in United States.

- Purchase almost 26 percent of kids' clothing.

- In the greeting card industry alone, seniors are the No. 1 greeting card purchaser because they may have two or three children, eight or nine grandchildren and dozens of nieces and nephews for whom to buy. They are at the top of the family pyramid in terms of family purchases.

- Providing age-based solutions offers unique opportunities to satisfy. For example, watching bank tellers communicate with 35-year-olds and 65-year-olds reinforces for me the insight service givers would derive from looking at the color of their customers' hair and the wrinkles on their brow rather than just their bank statements.

Research indicates that 35-year-olds are "time poor" — in a hurry, have more to do than hours in which to do it. They want their service providers to be quick—efficient—convenient. Actually they want service to be *very* quick—*very* efficient—*very* convenient.

On the other hand, sixty-five-year-olds have time. They want to enhance and enjoy time. Don't want to feel rushed.

Researchers have differentiated the attitude of the mature from the attitude of the young adult as follows:

Mature	Young Adult
■ *more introspective*	■ *more extroverted*
■ *perceive in shades of gray*	■ *perceive in black and/or white*
■ *more discretionary behavior*	■ *more unpredictable behavior*
■ *declining influence by peers*	■ *heavily peer influenced*
■ *more individualistic*	■ *more subordinated to others*

Why is it that many bank tellers communicate in the same uninterested mono-tone to both? Why is it that the salespeople in retail shops don't recognize the difference in their customers' gait? Why is it that corner traffic lights change at a predetermined speed rather than according to the age of the population in the area?

> *The older women of the future are going to be much more savvy and much more knowledgeable about everything financial.*
>
> Vicki Thomas, marketer

Near my home there is an intersection that frequently traps seniors with "the red" while they are in mid-crossing. Why is it that younger people assume that the aging process that creates gray hair, also creates stupidity? They often treat seniors like children. Why?

TARGET MARKETS BY LIFE CIRCUMSTANCES

In addition to age, a great many other life situations, such as affluence, poverty, education, disabilities and gender, influence our needs, our wants and affect our marketplace.

To please people is a great step towards persuading them.

Philip Dormar Stanhope, (1694-1773), English Secretary of State
Letters of Lord Chesterfield to His Son

THE AFFLUENT

Who are they?

- *American Demographics and Consumer Trends* considers U.S. households affluent at $50,000+ a year and "truly affluent" at $100,000 a year. Canadian sources consider households affluent at $70,000+ a year.

- $50,000 U.S. *(and $70,000 Canadian)* represent approximately 24 per cent of the population. While $100,000 U.S. *(and $140,000 Canadian)* represent approximately 4% of the population.

- account for almost 40 percent of the nation's wealth

- cross all geographic regions and ethnic boundaries

- well-educated, well-traveled

What do they want/need?
- *low key, unobtrusive luxury, inconspicuous consumption*
- *ease of travel*
- *vacation homes*
- *quality and value in clothing, furniture, cars, art, fine crafts, jewelry*
- *fine food, prepared at home or in restaurants*
- *healthy diet*
- *ease of living*
- *housekeeping services*
- *education*

- think of themselves as "upper middle class," rather than wealthy

How do you reach and satisfy them?

- network their trusted affinity groups

- get endorsements from their opinion leaders

- word of mouth

- referrals

- provide outstanding service

- ensure long term "value" in big purchases

- competitive pricing

Are you aware?

- Households headed by 35 to 54-years-olds are most likely to be affluent.

- Only 17 percent of households headed by someone under 35-years-old are affluent.

- Only 18 percent of households headed by someone 55 years and older are considered affluent.

- Twenty-two percent of housekeeping services such as house cleaning and gardening are purchased by this group.

- Tastes have changed. They are looking for things that set them apart from their neighbors, rather than consumables that are made by hand.

- Purchase at craft shows, auctions, studios.

- Collect glass, ceramic and other objets d'art.

- Live in two income households.

- Earn financial status through work — corporate, professional, entrepreneur. Many are now in "knowledge based" sector.

- Not big risk takers.

- Most feel it will be harder for younger generation to succeed financially.

What do they want/need?
- *empathy, sensitivity*
- *accessibility*
- *product adaptation, from clothes and food packaging to household appliances to transportation*
- *elimination of discrimination*
- *clear, consistent standards to address their needs*
- *require special consideration in several areas including: employment public services public transportation telecommunications*
- *require assistive technology*

DISABLED (WITH SOME DISABILITIES)

Who are they?

- growing market of 43 million Americans

- eight percent of the Canadian population *(over the age of 15)*

How do you reach and satisfy them?

- learn about and offer services to meet particular needs, regard them on an equal basis

- advocacy groups

- publications focused toward disabled

- create an environment that makes participation possible

- There is a divisive "us and them" attitude that must be overcome when regarding the disabled stated Bonnie Sherr Klein, award-winning documentary filmmaker and stroke victim, during a Canada AM *(Canadian morning TV news)* interview. She authored *Slow Dance*, an account of her recovery.

Are you aware?

- Wal-Mart offers employee training classes specifically for disabled.

- Home Access Design Inc., a Canadian builder , is constructing 100 percent accessible housing.

TARGET MARKETS BY GENDER

WOMEN

Who are they?

- sophisticated, informed shoppers who influence 70 percent of all buying decisions

- a diverse population

How do you reach and satisfy them?

- influencers, peer group leaders

- marketing geared to women *(print & electronic media)*

- relevant products and services that answer their concerns

What do they want/need?
- *value: high quality and low cost*
- *time savings*
- *relief from stress caused by their increased responsibilities (take care of both elderly parents and at-home or returned-to-home children)*
- *equality*
- *sense and sensitivity*

- solve their problems, alleviate their fears

- ease their responsibilities

- treat them as equals

- recognize the criteria they use to buy:

  - value: factory outlets and warehouse clubs, catalogs and TV home shopping

  - time savers: prepared foods, take-out

  - safety: hotel security, well-lit parking lots, house alarms

Are you aware?

- 41 percent of women's food budget is spent away from home.

- Women aged 45 to 54 will account for more than one-third of all net additions to workforce between 1995-2005.

- Women in senior management positions are vastly better educated than all women. Forty nine percent of them are in service industries.

- Households spend an average of $607 a year on women's clothing *($345 on men's clothing)*.

- The single largest clothing expense is for women's shoes *($121 a year)*.

- Women and men have different political orientations because their lives are different. The average female voter of the future will have different wants and needs than the average male voter.

MEN

Who are they?

- more sensitive and understanding than the "strong, silent type" of yesteryear

- sports enthusiasts

- consumers of newspapers, news shows

- buyers rather than browsers

What do they want/need?

- *information — do it your-selfers "must know"*
- *product knowledge*
- *to look good*
- *job security*
- *financial freedom*

How do you reach and satisfy them?

- influencers, peer group leaders

- marketing through preferred media: newspapers, TV, radio

- news programs and documentaries *(rather than award or game shows or sitcoms)*

- focus on their societal roles such as fatherhood or wage earners and their interests such as sports, gardening or house repairs

- focus marketing to information rather than emotion

- understand whether market group is "change adapters" or "change opposers" and market appropriately

A GQ magazine study classified these two groups of men and identified "change adapters" as younger, willing to try new things, experiment with new ideas. Not yet ready to marry and accept responsibilities.

"Change opposers" were identified as cautious spenders with

> *Men now see that they have choices to live different kinds of lives. This is healthy not only for them but also for the women in their lives. Men are no longer following prescribed patterns and getting boxed into pre-ordained behavioral habits.*
>
> Michael Clinton
> GQ

less money to spend. They engage in a great deal of background research before making a decision. Not brand loyal.

Are you aware?

- Spend 61 percent of food budget away from home.

- Do more shopping and housework than their fathers did.

- Dominate high-tech purchasing.

- Drink 85 percent of beer sold.

TARGET MARKETS BY ETHNICITY

Ethnicity, background, traditions, cultural values and former experiences also determine one's membership in specific target markets. The following ethnic groups represent large and growing markets. They are by no means the only ethnically targeted groups. Not discussed here, but also vital in determining North American target markets appropriate for your products or services because of their size, are the ethnic markets of Italians, Jews, French and Native Peoples, just to name a few.

AFRICAN-AMERICANS

Who are they?

- 12 percent of the American population

- an increasingly diverse group from poor to affluent

- 62 percent of families in U.S. earn less than $25,000 a year

- 12 percent of families earn more than $50,000 a year

- live mainly in large cities

- lower level of formal education than average

What do they want/need?

- *equality of opportunity*
- *increased educational opportunities*
- *recognition of identity, heritage*
- *equal pay for equal work*
- *equal opportunity for advancement*
- *respect*

- higher unemployment rate than average

- lower family income than average *(attributed to large number of households headed by women)*

- spend more than $170 billion annually

- family size is 3.49 people — which is larger than the average 3.17

How do you reach and satisfy them?

- address by earning power, household grouping, age as well as ethnic background

- recognize that affluent are moving out of center cities to suburbs — their needs are similar to other affluent groups

- utilize African-American publications

- utilize African-American role models, spokespeople

- ensure relevancy and empathy with publication for reader

- recognize distinct preferences in spending such as clothing and convertibles

- use television to reach teens but be aware that they mistrust the message because of its mainstream image

- use peer group leader for most credible influencer

Are you aware?

- African-American teens are very clothes and designer conscious.

- Only 56 percent are satisfied with their job.

- The gap between haves and have-nots is widening.

AFRICAN-CANADIANS

What do they want/need?
- *awareness for their roots, heritage and sense of identity*
- *associations hold an important place for group because they promote Black accomplishments*
- *hold onto cultural heritage—sense of the past and link it with present and future*

Who are they?

- less than one percent of the Canadian population

- comprised of both recent immigrants from Africa and long-time residents who left the United States to escape slavery

How do you reach and satisfy them?

- utilize group's own media including newspaper, TV and radio since it functions as its voice

CARIBBEAN-CANADIANS

Who are they?

- about 1.5 percent of the Canadian population

- residing primarily in Ontario and Quebec

- emigrated from Caribbean including Jamaica, Trinidad, Tobago, Haiti and Guyana

- 50 percent of group have ancestral roots in South Asia and India

- make up the majority of the Canadian Black community

What do they want/need?

- *the opportunity to maintain their Caribbean culture and sense of community, while participating in mainstream society*

- *recognition of their identity and heritage and the contribution they are able to make to society*

How do reach and satisfy them?

- utilize Caribbean-Canadian print publications as well as their own radio and TV programs

- offer products and services to which they are accustomed—which they want

- communicate with associations that promote Black culture

Are you aware?

- Group is made up of much ethnic and cultural diversity, so traditions vary significantly.

HISPANICS-AMERICANS

What do they want/need?

- *recognition of their cultural pride*
- *sensitivity to needs, heritage, language*
- *recognition of differences within the Hispanic community*
- *recent immigrants want to be addressed in Spanish, whereas U.S. born Hispanics want to be addressed in English*

Who are they?

- 10 percent of the U.S. population — growing at approximately five times the rate of the total U.S. population

- a diverse target — because of length of time in the United States and their reasons for emigrating from Central and South America

- less inter-marriage than other ethnic groups, slowing down assimilation and acculturation

- 72 percent expressed job satisfaction — highest of any race or ethnic group

- strong cultural values

- family-oriented

How do you reach and satisfy them?

- recognize that they are a complex, diverse target requiring a variety of communication options

- attract U.S. born Hispanics with English-speaking advertising, incorporating Latino culture

- attack the notion of a single Hispanic market through use of Spanish

- use TV as your medium of choice

- more than three-quarters of Hispanics surveyed by the

Hispanic MONITOR, watched or listened to Spanish language programming

- print is media used least

- recognize and learn about the differences and similarities of Hispanic and American cultures

- understand subtleties of this complex and diverse culture

Are you aware?

- Life expectancy is shorter (less than 70 years, as compared to general U.S. population of 75 years+).

- Hispanics are expected to become U.S.'s largest minority group in less than 15 years.

- Cultural pride is growing — moving Hispanics away from mainstream.

- 60 percent of Hispanics fall into modest or low-income groups.

- 14 percent of Hispanic households have an annual income of $50,000 or more.

- 60 percent of U.S. Hispanics have Mexican roots, 12 percent Puerto Rican and 5 percent Cuban.

HISPANIC-CANADIANS

Who are they?

- approximately 1.2 percent of the Canadian population

- seventh largest ethnic minority in Canada

- emigrated from Latin America and Spain

- family size—3.8 persons

How do you reach and satisfy them?

- use TV as a communication vehicle

- use community Spanish newspaper

Are you aware?

- 55 percent have post-secondary education

What do they want/need?
- *recognition that as a group they are not similar to U.S. Hispanics*
- *recognition of their educated status.*
- *realize they require a more entrepreneurial attitude to succeed*
- *job continuity*

ASIANS

Who are they?

- 3.5 percent of the American population

- 5.2 percent of the Canadian population

- impressive purchasing power

- maintain centuries-old traditions

- incorporate some North American culture

- primarily located in large cities

- high rate of business ownership

What do they want/need?
- *respect for tradition*
- *strong regard for learning*
- *products, services that "fit" into traditions*
- *traditional foods*
- *solidarity, support of group*

- high level of education

- more affluent than any other ethnic minority

- live predominantly in married couple households with two wage earners

How do you reach and satisfy them?

- understand and respect culture

- communicate appropriately through ethnic oriented media

- word of mouth

- development of trust

- use staff who speak their language

- consider the other target groups to which they also belong and incorporate in communication strategy

- consider age and how recently immigrated

- cater to smaller clothes sizes *(American sizes are too large)*

- understand their interest in maintaining community and the value they place on heritage

- segment by nationality *(Chinese, Japanese, Korean, etc.)*. Do not market to them as a single group.

- use print — newspapers in appropriate language

- a complex market that takes a long-term effort to successfully understand and unfold

Are you aware?

- fastest growing ethnic group in North America

Part three utilizes the marketing perspective to high-light the critical role differentiation plays in answering *"Why should someone do business with you...rather than someone else?"* The techniques to adopt a memorable theatrical approach are detailed. Included are the advantages of communicating dramatically, differentiating your products and services, merchandising effectively and encouraging customer participation, so you get and keep customers for the long term. A short explanation of GMROI, Gross Margin Return on Investment, a merchandising planning tool, and its advantages is included in the addendum.

Pursue Differentiation　　　3

What makes you and your organization different?

What makes you and your organization special?

How do you communicate that difference, that uniqueness?

At the corner of Yonge Street and Eglinton Avenue in Toronto, sit four banks, the Scotiabank, the TD (Toronto-Dominion), the CIBC (Canadian Imperial Bank of Commerce) and the Bank of Montreal. **What differentiates one from the other?** As a new resident to the area, **what would encourage you to choose one over the other?** As the bank manager, **what could you do to convince customers to bank with you rather than someone else?**

Your business is also fraught with competition. **How are you differentiating yourself?** *"Why should someone do business with you... rather than someone else?"*

Tomorrow, not one single thing of significance will occur in this nation — not one law will be passed, not one product purchased, not one management decision made, not one couple would get married — but that somebody had not sold a product, an idea or a concept to someone else. Marketing enables all other sophisticated human activity.

Lewis D. Eigen, Executive Vice President
University Research Corporation

In today's world blinded by overexposure, **how do you achieve these goals? How do you become better than you were yesterday? Better than your competition is today? How do you make and sell improved products and services better than you did yesterday? How do you communicate your benefits and advantages to the marketplace with passion, excitement, energy?**

Our overcrowded marketplace, inundated with look-alike products, talk-alike salespeople, do-alike services, flooded with false promises, and frequent disappointments, has made communicating believable benefits tougher than ever before! Tough, but not impossible.

CUT THROUGH THE CLUTTER

Ensure that your products, services, customer service, delivery, operations, customer support, added-value, stand out from the crowd. Become that single memorable, iridescent fish, swimming with a school of dull gray ones, by developing, communicating and implementing a marketing plan that reflects your iridescence.

Transitional times can be frightening, but differentiating yourself will direct you to a safe haven in a volatile marketplace. It can be a time for market share increase, company growth, horizon expansion for those who are willing to go against the grain.

Seize the opportunity to differentiate yourself in the marketplace, to differentiate your business from your competitors by looking at every aspect of your marketing. All the big things. All the little things.

IBM differentiated its product by offering technologically advanced assistance to a networked community. The reality of on-going electronic commerce prompted IBM to provide Cryptolopes(TM) with its improved security and encryption technology to Internet users, ensuring their messages are "for your eyes only."

Their infoSage software searches Cybermalls that are selling merchandise to customers on-line, to find your specific request. Decision making and planning are simplified. Your profits are increased.

Bayer differentiated itself from generic aspirin by including "trust," "reliability" and "experienced medicinal aid" into its offering. The pain-killer 222 has so successfully differentiated itself in Canada, that my wife swears she doesn't get the same relief from the drugstore generic equivalent.

Effective differentiation is not limited to customer needs and expectations. Often an "extra," something they never expected to receive, is the key to establishing a memorable position. When Chapters, one of the mega bookstores, opened in Toronto recently, I expected the comprehensive selection of books and the knowledgeable staff. However, I didn't expect the glorious library study tables and chairs that dot the store, encouraging me to rest and read — and eventually decide I just can't leave without buying.

> *Pull out all the stops.*
> *Find a "different way" to*
> *get applause.*
> Sam Geist

> *In the past you could enter markets at your own pace. Today you have to learn what customers want, make it and sell it, or someone else will.*
>
> E. Kirby Warren,
> Columbia University School of Business
> *The New York Times*

Develop and institute a plan that recognizes the value of your loyal customers. They are the lifeblood of your business. Vilfredo Pareto, the Italian philosopher and mathematician's 20/80 rule states that 20 percent of your customers generate 80 percent of your sales. That's a powerful incentive to keep them close. Seek out differentiating ways to do that.

Differentiation enables you to forge ahead. No, it forces you ahead. It separates you from those notoriously indistinguishable "Bobs" who all belong to the "Bob Club," — those think-alike, dress-alike, do-alike "Bobs" who look at each other, only to see themselves.

> *Don't forget that your product or service is not differentiated until the customer understands the difference.*
>
> Tom Peters, business writer
> *Thriving on Chaos*

The secret for success — for profitability — lies quite simply in differentiating yourself from everything that's out there. Start from the top and differentiate! Differentiate! Differentiate! all the way through your organization.

TAKE THE THEATRICAL APPROACH

On a recent visit to the ancient city of Ephesus, on the Aegean coast, I saw a very early example of advertising. There on the roadway just outside the remains of the library lies an inscribed tablet proclaiming the opportunity to be enjoyed by engaging a "Madam of the Night." Her message was clear. Her marketing, effective. The goal of marketing has changed little in the thousands of intervening years. Communicate. Involve. Get participation. It was expected then. It is expected now. Put on a performance so bold, so fresh, so thrilling, it demands response. Do it every day, in everything you do.

An excellent way to execute an arousing, stimulating, involving, differentiating marketing strategy is by using a theatrical approach. Transform your stage *(your store, your show-room, your business environment, your office, your factory)* into a Hollywood set filled with the excitement and fun customers have come to expect. You are in the entertainment business. Create theater.

It's not easy to deliver a hit performance every day, but since you're already in business, it makes good sense to polish up your production. Prepare for the longest run in history by demonstrating a theatrical "It's Showtime" attitude.

> *Theatrical marketing catches the imagination–it moves us to laugh–to participate–to act. It transports us to new heights by providing entertaining solutions. On stage as a marketer you must play a differentiating role–to be remembered–to be innovative–to be believed.*
>
> Sam Geist

> *The whole point of everything we do is to make the customer happy for the long haul. If people are satisfied and excited about the experience of shopping at Nordstrom, they will come back. And if you haven't created that atmosphere, they won't come back. It's just that simple.*
>
> David Lindsey, Vice president, store planning Nordstrom
> *The Nordstrom Way*, R. Spector & P.D. McCarthy

Create an experience your customers will always remember. Answer *"**Why someone should do business with you... rather than someone else?**"* five ways.

- *Communicate Dramatically*
- *Tour Your Theater*
- *Glamorize Your Oft-Forgotten Props*
- *Make Your Products And Services Legendary*
- *Stay Ahead of the Copycats*

COMMUNICATE DRAMATICALLY

Communicate with pizzazz on as many sensory levels as possible. We sometimes forget that customers use more than their sense of sight to make a purchase decision. We touch what we want to buy, we often smell, listen to and occasionally taste what we want to buy.

By incorporating as many sensory levels as possible in your marketing plan, you greatly increase the likelihood of involvement — of purchase.

People Remember
20 percent of what they hear.
30 percent of what they see.
50 percent of what they see and hear.
80 percent of what they do.
Edgar Dale, author & researcher

A study conducted by Drake and Washington State Universities concluded that shoppers return more often to scented stores. Customers perceive the merchandise to be of better quality. The researchers advice is to use aromatic candles or potpourri.

HMV, with record stores worldwide, includes customer "listening booths" in their music stores. At Whole Foods Market, an organic food chain, sampling and mood music courtesy of a professional cellist elevate a shopping trip to a memorable experience. Choosing furniture for a new home? Renovating an older home? New computer software assists in the selection or renovation process by allowing customers "to see" the finished results. With "virtual reality" they are actually able to "walk through," "sit down" and "touch" the purchases, long before they are actual reality.

Another interesting phenomenon to consider is that the effect achieved by involving additional senses to sight is greater than that achieved by using each sense alone. You are well aware of the incentive to buy when the fragrance of freshly baked bread wafts through the grocery store, or the inducement to relax in the dentist's chair when your headset fills you with classical music, or the temptation to participate at a games table when the lights flash, bells bong, the chips jingle and the crowd cheers. Involve all your customers' senses in an entertaining environment to create "wow," to ensure participation.

> *Who the hell wants to hear actors talk? [In 1927, considering the possibility of talking motion pictures]*
>
> Harry Warner, founder
> Warner Brothers Studio
> *The Experts Speak,* Cerf & Navasky

TOUR YOUR THEATER

Take an objective look around your "theater," showroom or factory, your store or office and determine **what makes and**

what could make your surroundings special, memorable, different from your competitors? Reflect the physical, visual representation of your aspirations, your dreams, hopes, goals and investment.

Successful marketers begin to tour their theater from the outside looking in. *First impressions last*. Start, where your customers start. Instead of entering through the employee entrance, walk through the front door and see what your customers see when they enter. Congratulate yourself on your bright inviting exterior, your spotless entrance, your enchanting window displays, your easy-to-read and understand signs. Become aware how all your senses are aroused as soon as you enter, just as your customers' senses would be. **Do the sounds and the sights excite you? Do you feel the hustle-bustle, the warmth, the subdued elegance, the off-the-wall excitement, the professionalism, the impression of value, the activities, the action? Are you experiencing what you want your customers to experience when they walk through your front door? Are you creating a differentiated environment that creates top-of-mind memorability and encourages loyalty? Are you creating an environment that shouts "It's Showtime" loud and clear?**

Are you creating the ambiance, the atmosphere, the feeling that is you? Owning an identifiable, positive, consistent, eye-catching position in your customer's mind is paramount in selling your organization and its merchandise and services to your customer. Your business is tangibilized by what is physically seen and remembered about you. It tells customers who you are. It tells them what you're selling *(quality, value)*, what your price point is, what your sense of customer is, what your marketplace position is *(remember the slogan "we're No. 2 so we try harder")*. And it tells them why they should do business with you rather than someone else. Think the golden arches, think Juan Valdez and his donkey, think Apple Computer Inc.'s "apple," think the Prudential rock.

Keep in mind that your customers are part of a dynamic, action filled marketplace with no geographical boundaries — a marketplace that is privy to the advantages of a rapidly shrinking global village. They expect innovation. They demand change.

Visiting an environment where nothing happens, where nothing changes from day to day, from year to year bores today's customers *(and staff)*. No one wants to patronize the same show forever. With so many opportunities for an entertaining experience, **what can you do to encourage customers to choose your theater? How can you create a dilemma for your customers?**

> *Create a dilemma for your customers. The dilemma of "which to buy" rather than "whether to buy." Turn browsers into shoppers.*
>
> Sam Geist

Visit other "theaters." Adapt the best of what you see. Look at other industries. Modify their successes to suit your requirements. Read trade journals, scan monthly magazines and out-of-town newspapers. They all provide innovative ideas to refresh your show.

Emulate Movenpick, a restaurant enterprise originating in Switzerland. They saw how customers got involved at country markets, how they enjoyed the sights, the sounds, the freshness. They re-created that outdoor market ambiance, with its sights, its sounds and its freshness in their Marché restaurants, most successfully. Customers line up nightly. They wander through the market and choose whatever fresh selections they fancy. It's prepared on the spot for them, to be enjoyed at one of the marketside tables.

Emulate Eatzis, a take-out deli originating in Dallas, Texas. Concept creator, Phil Romano, wanted to put on a "meals solution show" for his customers so in his Dallas location, he employs 43 chefs in full regalia, to prepare 6,000 meals-to-go, frontside. The supporting cast of 173 staff members offers customers tastings of everything in the store. Customers are eating it up and returning again and again, ensuring this show is a big hit!

You have real competition and opportunity! Re-evaluate your aspirations, dreams, hopes and plans on an on-going basis. Re-define your goals and objectives to reflect the market's changing wants and needs. Search out unexplored niches, discover unique benefits in order to be different, to be memorable.

Maintain a flexible approach, one that can easily accommodate surprise market developments or new competitive introductions. Often the idea of changing

> *Because its purpose is to create a customer, the business enterprise has two — and only these two basic functions: marketing and innovation. Marketing and innovation produce results; all the rest are "costs."*
>
> Peter F. Drucker, management consultant and writer
> *People and Performance*

(especially against the grain) — of moving forward from a tried-and-true position meets with resistance. Although it may take time, and cost money, not changing, *not* differentiating your marketing strategy can be far more expensive.

Differentiate! Differentiate dramatically!

Ask yourself **how do your customers feel in your theater, your store or office or showroom or factory? How do they feel after receiving your service? How do they feel after buying your products?**

They should feel satisfied, comfortable, stimulated to participate again. To a great extent their comfort is established and maintained because your image and your customers' image of themselves are in sync. This bond is developed primarily by visual clues.

Hold onto this bond. Changing the visual representation of who you are, especially when it's at odds with what your customers perceive, causes customer confusion. Confusion causes lack of comfort. Lack of comfort causes customer stress, separation and divorce.

Part of the dynamic, changing, living environment, is your ability to maintain the connection that inspired customer confidence and satisfaction in the first place. A trusted image can't be changed happily overnight.

Product manufacturers are well aware that they must differentiate their products, that they must update their products' taste or features and benefits to match their changing market. They also are very aware that they mustn't change who they are or what they represent.

U.S. department stores, such as Macy's and Burdines, undergo face-lifts regularly. They rejuvenate, modernize to reflect their changing market, but the merchandise mix, services offered, policies, customer privileges, core identity do not suddenly change *(unless of course, their strategies are unsuccessful)*. Coca-Cola has changed its logo numerous times over the decades. Yet each change was small, subtle. Never was there a doubt in their market's mind who Coke was and what they stood for.

> ### *If you don't know where you're going, stay where you are.*
> From the 1995 movie *Boys on the Side*

Altered subtly perhaps, but irrevocably gone, never. Well, almost never. Coke's misguided effort at irrevocable change will go down in the annals of marketing history, as a classic.

Customers' need for comfort is very real.

GLAMORIZE YOUR OFT-FORGOTTEN PROPS

Even though they are not the central characters of your production, the backdrop, the props perform valuable service. They alert your customers' senses to the whole scene. They broaden the scope, they add to the excitement, adventure, suspense. They heighten the fun, the drama.

A bare stage often results in sensory deprivation for the audience, and exerts enormous pressure on the actors *(your staff)* to carry the entire production on their own. Visual merchandising adds the music, the laughter, the drama, to your business. It encourages customer involvement. Excellent visual merchandising helps you stage a held-over hit everytime. In addition to setting the mood, effective merchandising also serves a very functional role. It assists customers to easily find what they are looking for, *(just like row and seat numbers in the theater speedily directs the audience to their places)* thereby encouraging and facilitating the sale.

By building a well laid out set, you assist your staff in giving superior performances and you assist your customers in enjoying the show all the more.

Barnes & Noble CEO, Leonard Riggio realized the benefits of ensuring his audience enjoyed the dazzle of the show by incorporating the traditional library atmosphere *(for book lovers);* modern styling, graphics and displays *(for theater goers);* warm public meeting space *(for everyone).* He hired approachable actors *(staff)* to complete the scene.

Consider these 10 visual merchandising suggestions, compiled by visual merchandising experts, to enhance your business environment.

1.   Do a reality check of your outside signs.

What you manage to observe in about six seconds is what your customers see as they pass your location. That's all the time they give to letting your outside signs register. If location is a problem, directive signs shouldn't be.

While vacationing in Florida, my wife and I heard radio advertising for a new discount women's wear store. The commercial gave directions. Only after we had driven around for ages, had given up ever finding the store and had turned around to go back home, did we notice a small sign off in the distance that gave a clue to its location. Lest you think I'm just no good at directions, once inside, we heard the phone ring several times from other customers who needed assistance with the directions.

Customers don't want their experiences to be unpleasantly complicated. *(Besides, after becoming discouraged and upset about not finding the location, what's their mood like when they finally do come in. Is it conducive to buying?)*

2. Merchandise from your customers' viewpoint.

Two well-known gourmet food emporia, Balducci's in New York City and Pusateri's in Toronto, must have stood *first* in their visual merchandising class. They surround their customers with the sights, sounds, smells and tastes that directly precede the sales.

3. Sign with graphics.

Graphics visually differentiate. They're memorable. They assist to identify your business. At Lake Tahoe, there is a small mall where each store is identified by a beautiful, hand-carved, hand-painted sign. The message conveyed to shoppers is one of quality, care, personal service from people who take such pride in their stores they invest in such original signs.

If your logo can be graphically represented, all the better, it will be easily identified. Product manufacturers have been using graphics as identity markers for years; the shape of the Coke bottle, the shape of the Heinz ketchup label, the Gerber baby, the B.F. Goodrich tire, the Campbell's soup kids make them memorable. Service givers also use graphics to "tangibilize" their services — the Allstate hands, the RE/MAX *(a world-wide realty company)* balloon, and the Shoppers Drug Mart *(Canadian and Israeli)* prescription symbol, are all recognizable and memorable.

4. Keep it inviting.

Visual merchandising should be easy on the eye, easy on the brain. An assault on the senses usually leads to customer withdrawal, whether it's intrusive sound *(music blasting, constant intercom announcements)*, unpleasant smells or distracting sights *(flashing lights, overloaded visuals)* or uncomfortable temperatures.

Keep it inviting! If it's so fragile, they're afraid to touch, if it's so dark they can't see the menu, if it's so high they can't reach the merchandise, if it's so awkward they can't open or close the Jeep's trunk door, they won't try, they won't buy.

Keep it inviting, keep it comfortable by training staff to make service announcements such as "plumbing associate to aisle four" sound as if the customer is about to receive added value service. Too often it sounds like a panic stricken plea for help from anyone within earshot.

Keep it inviting refers not only to the retail scene, but also to the waiting rooms and meeting rooms of businesses and professionals where often it is too hot or too cold, the TV is too loud, the seating arrangements uncomfortable and the magazines pre-date this decade.

Creators of Web sites have taken the "keep it inviting" to heart. They realize a clear and accessible layout, with information that is updated daily, encourages return visits. Computer software creators develop program packages with "user friendly" in mind as well to ensure interest and involvement.

5. Make your merchandise and services your main attraction.

> *70 percent of a buying decision is made on the floor of the store.*
>
> Michael Wahl, author
> *In Store Marketing*

Your customers want to buy, want to participate. That's why they come. I always think of Crate & Barrel and The Pottery Barn when I think of outstanding merchandising. My wife goes in to enjoy the atmosphere and the inviting displays. She wants to buy *(and usually succeeds)*. I always think of my kids' orthodontist, Dr. Shapera when I think of outstanding merchandising. My kids actually wanted to go. They enjoyed seeing *(and playing with)* his ever-changing displays.

6. Color-code.

Color identifies, speeds up recognition. Color-code by department, by category, by size, by fashion grouping. Airports with several terminals color-code the terminals and the pathways within them to enhance the traffic flow.

Color-coding from a merchandising point of view assists customers purchase several items at a time more easily. The Gap merchandises its stores by color, rather than size, as do many other fashion retailers.

Color-coding a store from an aesthetic point of view not only provides consistency and familiarity but also creates image. The White House, an American women's fashion and accessory chain for example, built its business on the use of white.

7. Control customer traffic patterns.

Visual merchandising should create a series of focal points to encourage customers to travel through at their own pace, comfortably. It shouldn't confuse or deceive. Ikea, the Swedish-for-common-sense home store, realized this as it leads its customers very deliberately through the entire store, before they can exit past the cashiers. Walt Disney realized this as line-ups at Disneyland always seem to be moving, going somewhere special. The more effectively the layout is designed, the longer the customer will happily remain, and the longer they stay, the more....

8. Packaging is visual merchandising. Utilize it!

To a consumer, very often the packaging is the product. *(Think Tide, think the Republic of Tea's graphically memorable tea canister, think the recognizable around the world Diet Coke can, etc.).* It introduces the product and its advantages. It speaks of image, attitude, value and convenience. Product manufacturers, well aware of the function their packaging serves, develop it with great care, to gain shelf space, recognition and memorability.

Service givers are no less vulnerable to the impact of their packaging. Dentists' shingles introduce them. Their offices reinforce the feelings of trust and confidence or fear and hesitancy, long before their drill touches your teeth.

In a retail environment you are not only what your customers see inside the store, but what they take with them when they leave.

At Exquisite, a gift shop in southwest Florida, each purchase is beautifully wrapped in a bag, stuffed with pink and teal tissue and tied with pink and teal ribbons. When purchasing for yourself, you really have given yourself a gift. When it's for a friend, it's ready to give.

Macy's offers "collector" shopping bags, designed tastefully enough to use again and again.

The Style Design Shop, on Florida's east coast wraps in environmentally-friendly brown paper and trendy raffia. Its upscale image, enhanced by its visual merchandising, walks right out the door with its customers.

9. Create an environment.

Create an experience that customers want to come to time and again. Whether it is a masterful Walt Disney adventure like Fantasyland or Magic Mountain or a retail one like Macy's "The Cellar" or Chuck E. Cheese, maximize your visual merchandising for maximum results.

Differentiating your merchandising efforts certainly includes effective product placement. Grocery store mavens like Chris Thompson of Hartman's Your Independent Grocer in Ottawa and Ed Wowchuk of Main Street Payfair in Winnipeg strategically created a baby department to maximize sales potential of baby-related products. They discovered when everything for baby is merchandised together, chances are customers see *(and purchase)* additional items they forgot or hadn't thought of. Customers are also able to find what they want quickly, so it's easier for them to buy. And they do. Sales of baby products have substantially increased, as have sales on higher margin baby products for Thompson and Wowchuck, just because they're in sight.

An excellent way to determine if your merchandising efforts are as effective as you think is to obtain customer feedback. While the effectiveness or ineffectiveness of merchandising is most obvious at the retail level, it certainly affects guest *(no matter whether you call them customers, clients or patients)* comfort in professional offices and public environments, such as doctors' and dentists' offices, government buildings, hotels and airports. Create a simple questionnaire for customers to fill out and encourage response by offering an incentive.

10. Collect feedback.

An effective questionnaire is short and to the point. Give customers an opportunity to explain themselves and include comments, in addition to just checking off boxes.

The following questions have proved very helpful in acquiring information to determine merchandising effectiveness in a retail environment. They may be useful in assisting you develop a questionnaire that is appropriate to your own needs.

1. **Did you come to the store with a specific purchase in mind?**

2. **If yes, did you find it? How long did it take?**

3. **Did you need assistance locating it?**

4. **Did you notice anything else of interest while you were in the store?**

5. **If yes, what attracted you to it? Did you buy it?**

6. **What do you like best about our merchandise layout? Our displays?**

7. **How can we merchandise to make it easier for you to shop?**

8. **Please make any other comments you feel would help us help you better.**

Once you have perused a couple dozen feedback forms you will notice some comments are repeated. This will direct your attention to the areas that need improvement and the areas that are performing well.

Once the overall results are in, go to it. Re-merchandise, re-fresh. Differentiate your environment. Make it more entertaining. Make it more customer friendly than it has ever been before. Make it easier to buy, to obtain services.

MAKE YOUR PRODUCTS AND SERVICES LEGENDARY

Legends tend to be a little larger than life, recognized with awe, remembered with nostalgia. By differentiating your products, by differentiating your services, you make them more desirable. Work with manufacturers, distributors, service resources to enhance your product and service offerings, to make them impressive. By the time the competition has caught up *(and they will try)* you will be differentiating yourself with new and enhanced products and services.

One of the most powerful and profitable way to differentiate yourself is to apply Pareto's 20/80 principle to the merchandising of your products and services.

Since this concept is applicable primarily, but certainly not exclusively, to the retail community, I have included a discussion of it

When you design a product that flies off the shelves, it's just a matter of time before somebody copies it.

Francis Goldwyn, President
Manhattan Toy Co. Ltd.
Working Women

> **Sell solutions, not just products.**
>
> Klaus M. Leisinger, department director
> Ciba-Geigy Ltd.
> *The New York Times*

and of GMROI, an outstanding merchandise planning tool, as an addendum to this section, beginning on page 132.

Dave Nichols, former president of the Loblaws grocery chain kept the entire Canadian food industry on its toes as he introduced, with lightning speed, one innovative product after another. No one could keep pace as he created powerful brand name awareness for his private President's Choice products such as his Decadent Chocolate Chip Cookies and his exotic Memories sauces, until they occupied a great percentage of valuable grocery shelf real estate, at excellent profit margins for Loblaws.

Create legendary product or service status even when the competition carries the same products or performs the same services by communicating more relevant information about those products and services than anyone else. Today's customers are thirsty for information. Provide it to satisfy them and bring them back.

Let customers know "What's in it for me?" on a regular basis. By really knowing your products or services well, you not only beneficially differentiate yourself from your competitors, you also achieve that much coveted expert status.

Communicate all three elements of every product and service. Market them clearly and advantageously.

Outline the features.

All the things to be seen, heard, tasted, smelled, felt by the product or service. Customers want to know about colors, sizes, fabrics, special features, cost.

Highlight the attributes.

All the things the features do. Their capabilities. Customers need to know how it works, about the warranties and guarantees.

Detail the benefits.

All the things the features and attributes do for your customers. The advantages. Customers listen to WIFM (*"What's In It For Me?"*) all the time.

Their purchase decisions pivot on WIFM . By detailing the benefits effectively, you assist customers to clearly visualize how your products and services will help them and will change their lives for the better.

Charles Revson founder of Revlon said it succinctly years ago, *"In the factory we make cosmetics, in the store we sell hope."* Customers don't buy features and attributes, they buy benefits. They buy hope. Turn every product or service you have into a benefit. Market your product and service benefits with daring, with differentiation, with drama, with entertainment.

> *The real issue is value, not price.*
> Robert T. Lindgren
> Cross & Trecker Corporation
> *Harvard Business Review*

Let your customers know how your products and services will:

- *save them time*

- *give them value, enjoyment, pleasure, recognition*

- *eliminate their hassle, worry, problems, pain, stress, frustration*

- *provide peace of mind, satisfaction, pleasure*

- *make them feel good about themselves and the buying decision they have made.*

Offer these benefits and you will be appreciated, remembered, thought of first. Offer these benefits and your customers will recognize and applaud your products and services. Offer these benefits and you will build a powerful, lasting relationship with your customers.

1. Take an Innovative Approach.

Look at each situation from several different points of view, enabling you to find more than one solution to the inevitable challenges you face everyday.

Nothing is more dangerous than an idea when it is the only one you have.

Emile Chartier (Alain), (1868-1951),
French philosopher & essayist
A Whack on the Side of the Head, Oech

In their search for a new advertising agency, Purolator Courier Ltd., based in Toronto, put its bid on its Web site. Maurice Levy, senior vice-president of sales and marketing, had both practical and future-focused motives for the move. He felt by including all needed requirements on the Net his staff would be spared calls for information. As well, he said, "We are very much a technology company. Therefore, we wanted to deal with an agency that understands that medium. We figured this would be a good way to help evaluate the agency and help them evaluate our site." That's innovation — 1990s style.

> *We must compete in new ways if we are to prosper.*
>
> Thomas G. Plaskett, CEO
> Pan Am
> (Telex to employees)

Be open to new ideas. Keep an idea file so you'll remember to use them. Grow ideas, share ideas, adapt them.

Create marketing efforts that are so innovative that they become etched in the customer's brain. This marketing breaks out of the traditional mold. It is unique, remarkable, involving. Use a differentiated perspective to search out unique opportunities — undiscovered "holes." Look for "the hole" and fill it with a distinct, memorable plan of action.

As a marketer, fill "the hole" with differentiating benefits. Provide your customers with the unique benefits that doing business with you offers them. Communicate these benefits with daring. This approach provides an outstanding competitive advantage.

Remember, customers buy...

- *your benefits, not your products or services.*
- *the promises you make, so make them with care.*
- *your honesty, your integrity, your credibility.*

- *solutions to their desire for ease, success, security, love and belonging.*

- *consistency you've shown.*

- *value, which isn't the same as low price.*

- *selection and choice.*

- *freedom from risk, demonstrated by your warranty, guarantee and reputation.*

- *your image created by the media you use and the message you communicate to market yourself.*

- *expectations and beliefs based on your marketing efforts.*

- *solutions to their problems.*

Consider, for example, the marketing efforts of an organization like Target, an American mass merchandiser. In everything it does, in all its internal and external communications, it conveys its interest in and concern for its customers and for its customers' community, environment, society.

> *...a company's most precious asset is its relationship with its customers. It is not "who you know" but how well you are known to them.*
>
> Theodore Levitt, editor and writer
> Harvard Business School
> *The Marketing Imagination*

Whether at the store or in the media, the message is consistent. "We are part of your community. Your concerns, your challenges are our own — and as family we are doing whatever we can to answer your personal and community needs." Their message is believed.

2. Make Customers Feel Good

So much has changed since Henry Ford said of his Model T, as it came off the assembly line, *"They can have it in any color they want as long as it's black."* Today customers' needs, wants, satisfactions come first. In order to ensure your marketing plan matches your customers, you must talk to them. In order to offer them your benefits package, you must find out what they really want, what makes them feel good and then, give it to them.

Michael LeBoeuf, author of *How To Win Customers And Keep Them For Life*, clearly illustrated this concept with this vignette.

> *Jane, recently married, was having lunch with a friend, explaining why she married Bill instead of Bob.*
>
> *"Bob is Mr. Everything," Jane said, "He's intelligent, clever and has a very successful career. In fact when I was with Bob, I felt like he was the most wonderful person in the world."*
>
> *"Then why did you marry Bill?" her friend asked.*
>
> *Jane replied, "Because when I'm with Bill, I feel like I'm the most wonderful person in the world."*

That's it in a nutshell. People — your customers — want to feel good about themselves. They want to feel important, satisfied, pampered, helped. They want to feel good in their relationships with their family and friends. They want to feel good in their relationships with their business associates.

Marketing is a bigger adventure than it has ever been before.

Not only is it necessary to market your existing products and services well, it is also vital to be ever seeking new products and services to market — finding solutions that only a short while ago seemed improbable or unlikely.

George Gilmore, president of Moore Business Systems (MBS) in Canada, realized his customers wanted more than just business forms, the traditional product his company had provided for years. What his customers really needed were solutions to their information needs. Many of his clients, now electronically oriented, required help incorporating an electronic form system in their businesses. Others wanted simplification of their entire business form process. Shifting from a paper business form provider, to a supplier of information services, Moore Business Systems now sells the solutions its customers want and need. At MBS, internal re-organization, new job descriptions, new skills, overhauled marketing strategy, have all been successfully *(and profitably)* revised to meet today's needs and to offer today's benefits. Its customers are satisfied because their problems are solved.

3. **Satisfy A Niche Market.**

Provide new solutions by seeking out and satisfying a specialized niche. Instead of remaining a little fish in a big pond, consider the option of becoming a big fish in a small, and growing pond. Randy Sutton, owner of a Dallas, Texas bakery did. As a baker of regular bakery items, he was just one of the pack vying for customer attention. However, when he developed a line of sugar-free and fat-free baked goods, he found he could do very well in the growing diabetic and reduced-calorie market. Not only did this niche provide additional revenue, it also

> ***The name of the game is new products.***
>
> Michael Shrimi, CFO
> Bortz Chocolate Novelties, Inc.
> *The New York Times*

strengthened his sales of regular bakery lines. Retailers who purchased from his competitors now talk to him, because he has products no one else does.

Although John Kelly, chairman, CEO and president of Alaska Airlines is always on the lookout for new opportunities, he is very satisfied with the growth of *his niche market*—the north-south routes on the U.S. west coast, linking Seattle with California and Alaska—serving 10 million passengers in 1996. Alaska Airlines may not be the biggest or the best known, but they are consistently profitable.

Even entertainers, who we feel abide by rules of their own, must focus on their market, provide solutions, look for new niches, change, move with the times if they are to survive.

Clive Davis who, oversaw Whitney Houston's rise, says a star's longevity requires high-maintenance focus.

He commented, in *USA Today,* "If you're an entertainer in the tradition of Barbra Streisand or Whitney, you've got to keep diversifying and reinventing yourself. You can't stop growing and fall into a predictable formula. If you give the public exactly what it expects, you get boring." He could have easily included Madonna in his remarks.

Never stop stretching. Never stop listening. Never stop changing. Vital to Barbra and Whitney and Madonna — certainly vital to you.

The last seven words of a dying business, *"We've never done it that way before"* are worth repeating. Grow a new attitude. Observe from a new vantage point. Develop a point of difference. Adopt it aggressively. Use your marketing strategy to pass your competition. "As good as," *isn't.* Take some risks and create the hook that catches the marketplace.

4. **Communicate Tangibility and Intangibility.**

One of the seldom realized requisites for accurate communication is recognizing that all products and services have an element of intangibility about them. Products and services contain an element we can't experience before we use them. While the product/service itself is certainly tangible, its performance *(in essence the real reason we purchase)* sometimes remains elusive. We are often asked to buy promises — promises of performance — promises of satisfaction.

An example comes to mind. Driving down a country road you see a professionally printed sign that states: *"farm fresh eggs at the farmhouse on the left".* You debate as you drive and pass another sign, this one meticulously hand-lettered complete with hand-illustrated eggs in a basket: *"farm fresh eggs at the farmhouse on the right."* **Which sign would you heed? Where**

would you buy the eggs? Why?

Let's do a retake. This time as you are driving down the road you see a professionally printed sign that reads: *"Flying lessons available at the left."* You debate as you drive and pass another sign, *"Flying lessons available at the right,"* this one meticulously hand-lettered complete with an illustration of a plane. **Which sign would you heed? Where would you go for flying lessons? Why?**

Everyone requires risk-reducing reassurances from tangibles. Some tangibles require more reassurance than others.

Very often packaging is used to convey the promises implied, successfully or unsuccessfully, depending if we believe. The product or service benefits that are outlined, its design, its product name, the colors used, the appearance of the brochure all work to re-enforce the promises made by the product or service.

In the market for a new face cream? The name *Enliven*, in its feminine script intrigues. The copy promises younger looking skin thanks to medical breakthrough ingredients. It assures results that can be seen in a week. It guarantees money-back satisfaction. Promises. Promises. The package is shiny, creamy white. The lettering is raised gold print. The look is luxurious, refined, alluring. Promises. Promises. You buy those promises of satisfaction.

> *Presenting a professional, upbeat face to the public does wonders for the way people perceive your business.*
>
> Steve Estridge, CEO
> Temps & Co.
> *Inc.*

Tangible products must promise more than just features, more than just physicality — more than "the cream" or "the car" or "the cola" or "the vacuum cleaner." They must also promise the benefits to be derived by their purchase. Good marketers realize that tangibles must be beneficially "intangibilized" to increase customer interest and desire.

Intangibles on the other hand require some "tangibilization" since their satisfaction is mute. Their existence is recognized only by its absence.

Customers seldom realize what they are getting until they stop getting it. You are unlikely to be very conscious of good service in a restaurant. It's expected. It's only when the service is poor that you are aware of its absence. Consider other services to which you subscribe regularly and take for granted: banking services, cleaning services, maintenance services.

You expect satisfactory performance. You seldom *(if ever)* applaud when your monthly bank statement arrives *on time* — or when your shirts come back from the cleaners, *clean* — or when the waste baskets are emptied, carpets vacuumed, plants dusted and toilets cleaned at the office — or when the lights in the lobby of your apartment complex work. But, when these take-'em-for-granted expectations aren't there, you notice. You are not satisfied. You are not happy. "Tangibilizing" these intangibles is necessary.

To make customers aware of the intangibles you offer, create a tangible representation. For example the uniform you wear, the clipboard you carry, the clarity of your expression, your understanding of the task at hand give credence to your ability to repair the dishwasher or fix the furnace or conduct the computer training. Your appearance, your demeanor "tangibilizes" the intangible service before it is performed.

Josh, my 22 year-old son, travels across Canada, in his role as an outsourced Apple Computer trainer, conducting programs for the staff of many large computer dealers. His position requires trust, respect and attention from those attending, no matter *their* position or age. He gets it by the intangibles he offers — honed skills, updated knowledge, professional demeanor that fits his position, rather than speaks about his age.

To keep customers aware of the intangibles you offer, remind them of what they are receiving. Communicate regularly to build a positive relationship based on satisfaction. Communicating, or providing services only when there is a problem, opens the possibility for competitive interference in the meantime. At the very least, it allows the customer to enter into a relationship with someone else, because during the time they

Not very many years ago, professionals could count on their reputation and country club contacts to obtain a steady stream of clients or patients. Today, though, lawyers, accountants, management consultants, architects, engineers, dentists, doctors, and other professionals must do extensive marketing to maintain and build their practices. Two increasingly popular choices for educating and "comforting" buyers are seminars and newsletters.

Paul N. Bloom,
University of Maryland
Harvard Business Review

heard nothing from you, they did hear about your competitor from a close friend.

It is necessary for marketers of intangibles to solidify their presence and re-affirm their performance in the minds of their customers by reminding them of their existence and of the value of their service while it is being consistently, albeit silently, provided.

Send letters and update reports, prepare newsletters, make phone calls on a regular basis. These tangible reminders have enormous value.

Would you [want to] persuade, speak of interest, not of reason.

Benjamin Franklin, (1706-1790),
American printer & statesman
Poor Richard's Almanac

I would be remiss if I didn't mention Susie Bellina in this regard. She is a real estate agent who sells condos in a west coast Florida development. On a regular basis *(certainly monthly, perhaps more frequently)*, she sends updates of what is going on in the development and in the area. She occasionally includes photos and tidbits of news she feels would be of interest to owners in the development as well as highlights of real estate news. Her letters "tangibilize" her service. She is memorable. She works at building relationships so that when anyone who receives her mailings is interested in buying or selling real estate, who would they call? Susie Bellina!

Make your products and your services larger than life. Everyone loves a star.

STAY AHEAD OF THE COPYCATS

Imitation may be the sincerest form of flattery, but when copycats invade your territory, you wish they'd imitate someone else. Market leadership is maintained by staying ahead — being aggressive — taking action.

Consider each of the following eight proven techniques within the parameters of your own situation, translating the suggestions into applicable options. Keep at the forefront of your action plan how these benefits will satisfactorily answer *"Why should someone [continue to] do business with you...rather than someone else?"*

1. **Stress quality.**

   Excellent quality is an unbeatable advantage because it is a tangible benefit *(lives up to expectations, no hassles)*. When the quality of your products or services are enjoyed by your customers, it's difficult for a copycat to drive a wedge into your market share. It's only when your quality is in contention that look-alikes have an opportunity.

   General Motors maintained a huge market share lead for years based on the quality of their automobiles. It was only after their quality began to slip that Japanese car manufacturers managed to surge ahead, gaining enormous market share.

2. **Add value.**

   Larger size has become a common means lately for fast food chains to exude value. Bonuses offer another "value plus" avenue whether the bonuses are attached to the product, or are in combination with a partner *(of excellent reputation)* or are to be redeemed by mail.

Frequently two leaders get together to offer "special value" that capitalizes on their marketplace positions, re-verifies their reputations and ultimately suppresses the offerings made by copycats. Subway offers better value sandwich meals with Frito-Lay chips; Swiss Chalet, a Canadian chicken restaurant franchise, uses Toblerone chocolate to sweeten up their meal while American Express works fervently with entertainment venues to put its customers at the front of the line.

> **In my view he who goes ahead is always the one who wins.**
>
> Catherine The Great, (1729-1796)
> Empress of Russia
> *Correspondence with Baron F. M. Grimm*

If at all possible, choose a "value plus" that is in your customers interest and more difficult to emulate. UPS offers a direct on-line link between organizations and itself. By simplifying and speeding up service it adds value. Customers are able to track their packages, arrange pick-up and calculate shipping costs from their computers — and access customer service via e-mail.

3. Innovate.

Cater to your customers desire for more, or faster or lighter. *New! Improved!* is the marketing call for everything from detergent to contact lenses to no-fat yogurt to increase *(or just hold)* market share. Rapid and frequent product and service enhancements and re-designs leave copycats behind.

Today, technological leadership is a big advantage. Sony anticipated customer needs with the introduction of the Walkman personal tape player. By the time competitors got into the game, Sony was already marketing improved versions.

According to Dr. Thomas Robertson, professor of marketing at the London Business School, organizations looking for an innovative market strategy should be anticipating where customers needs will evolve, rather than focusing on current customer needs alone.

4. **Research and development.**

Especially when it's based on scientific research, new developments add credibility to your product, often initiating and sustaining market frenzy.

On the shelves of drug and health food stores for years, Vitamin E recently received a major boost when research determined a regular daily dose improved health and longevity. It has been almost impossible to keep the capsules in stock ever since.

5. **Clone near versions of the original.**

Replicate the original product or service, but with a new twist. This occurs constantly in the food industry to gain shelf space and weed out copycats.

Create demand.

Charles Revson, founder
Revlon
Watchwords to Managers

Versions with fruit and nuts, low or no fat versions, chocolate versions, hot, medium and mild versions, barbecued, salt &

vinegar, sour cream and onion versions of everything from cereals to salsas to potato chips share space with the original.

The electronic industry has also capitalized on the version method to increase market share and squeeze competition. Sharp Electronics has come out with a myriad of versions of its original "pocket organizer," each with innovative features that boggle the less computer-literate mind.

6. Create another niche.

Broaden your target market by providing customized products or services that appeal to additional market groups. This technique serves to further differentiate you and your offering from the copycats.

Huggies and Pampers, major brand name diaper suppliers, broadened their market appeal by creating versions targeted to specific niches. They offer extra absorbent diapers *(emphasizing their benefits),* ultra-trim fit diapers *(again stressing benefits),* fashion diapers in prints and designs geared for both boys and girls. With each product addition to match the needs of another market group, they were able to exploit new specific market niches and enlarge their target market. It should be noted, however, that in the diaper business, as in many other product areas, generics ride on the coattails of brand names, since they also have a loyal following: those consumers to whom price is the major determinant in purchase.

7. Give superior customer service.

It is here that many copycats fall short, primarily because they haven't built the infrastructure required to give effective and continuous customer support into their business. Today's marketplace leaders maintain their position by offering technical support. They staff phone lines with qualified, capable staff who quickly and correctly answer customer queries. They have R&D departments that can check problems and provide effective solutions. They communicate with their markets on an ongoing basis through newsletters and on the Internet utilizing Web sites to inform and update their customers, as well as solidify their relationship with them. Apple Computer, Inc. provides professional support and training for its Mac users. Its technical support team man phone lines to answer hardware problems ensuring that its computers remain user friendly and its customers remain satisfied and loyal.

8. Communicate your benefits — differently.

Years ago, hawkers at carnivals mesmerized open mouthed audiences with the incredible feats that awaited them behind the side show curtain. They were good. They were convincing. Their spiel hypnotized. We paid our 10 cents and went in to see the show. They, however, didn't have a whole lot of competition. Today's hawkers have much more.

Create good reasons and communicate new benefits to

encourage consumers to do business with you, rather than someone else. Tell them why they should pass three stores or three factories or three suppliers or three electricians offering identical products or services, to patronize you — why they should exchange their hard earned dollars for your products and services.

Every ad, every piece of direct mail, piece of literature, brochure, every commercial, cross-promotion, every community and charity involvement carries your personal stamp. Ensure that your message is clear. Ensure it is consistent with your market, their needs, expectations, desires. Ensure your message shouts benefits, promises, solutions. Be memorable, daring, dramatic. Tell your customers about your years of experience, your knowledge and expertise, your unique products, your value-rich extras, your consistent follow-up. Call your customers regularly. Invite them to special events. Encourage them to bring friends, come often, buy more.

Dick and Bev Keller operate Keller Foods, a supermarket in the tourist town of Banff, Alberta. Wanting a larger location *(they were doing well)* they moved just off the main street. Unexpectedly they found they were faced with the huge task of rebuilding their customer base. They put together a plan, a first rate production that is still running to ever increasing audiences.

They held draws for prizes donated by suppliers and used the names on the ballots to develop a well-targeted mailing list. They advertised and promoted to the list.

Recognizing that they draw tourists from around the world, they ensure their staff is able to serve in different languages. (*All told, their staff speaks at least six languages*).

Recognizing that their tourist market has special food interests, they carry a wide selection of ethnic products.

Realizing also that many of the tourists are health conscious teens or Generation Xers with limited budgets, they merchandise trays of prepared veggies with tubs of dip, in the produce department, ready to munch.

Recognizing that quality is an excellent differentiator they sell only aged, hung beef rather than the pre-packaged stuff sold by competitors.

They added value to a Keller's shopping experience.

Their marketing strategy, methodically developed, continues to be refined.

They realize "It's Showtime!" or nothing.

Marketing, like the operations or buying or distribution aspects of your business, is not a project —*it is a process*. It is never, ever finished.

As your greatest show on earth is about to begin, ask and answer those critical

> *Foreign managers take marketing seriously. In most American companies marketing still means no more than systematic selling. Foreigners today have absorbed more fully the true meaning of marketing: knowing what is value for the customer.*
>
> Peter F. Drucker, management consultant and writer
> *The Changing World of the Executive*

questions: **What makes you special? Different from your competitors? "Why should somebody do business with you...rather than someone else?"**

Don't let marketing opportunities escape! Always be on the lookout for new means to communicate. The Internet with its World Wide Web has opened huge opportunities for even the smallest companies. Reach out to a world of mass micro-marketing.

While buying a car is still a face-to-face experience, a large number of Internet sites offer helpful information to Net browsers. Everything from pricing guides to the features of specific models to the promises to get almost any make and model for factory prices is only a click away.

Communicate to your loyal "subscribers" regularly. They are vital to the longevity of your production. Offer them incentives to come in more often, purchase more, bring their friends.

Note their changing interests — their changing tastes — their changing needs. Satisfy them. *Satisfy them all.*

The information highway will change the whole idea of markets, because anybody with something to sell could be on an electronic network reaching people all over the world and accessing all kinds of information.

Bill Gates, CEO
Microsoft
Information Week

"Why should someone do business with you...rather than someone else?"

ASK. ANSWER. PLAN. CHANGE.

Use these questions and answers to help you develop a differentiating marketing strategy for today, *for tomorrow.*

1. **Why should somebody do business with you...rather than someone else?**

_____

_____

_____

_____

2. **What makes you — your organization different from your competitors?**

_____

_____

_____

_____

3. **What is your competitive advantage? How do you know? How can you increase your competitive advantage?**

_____

_____

_____

_____

4. Would you buy from you? Why? Why not?
   Would you do business with you? Why? Why not?

_____

_____

_____

_____

5. What "extras" have you incorporated into your marketing
   plan to increase your differentiation?

_____

_____

_____

_____

6. What can you change today in your marketing plan to
   create a theatrical approach?

_____

_____

_____

_____

7. On how many sensory levels do you communicate
   with your customers? What can you do to increase it?

_____

_____

_____

_____

8. What was your first impression of your organization when you walked through your customers' entrance? What can you do to create an even more positive impression?

_____

_____

_____

_____

_____

9. What have you included in your marketing plan to ensure your audience is comfortable, satisfied, interested in participating? What have you included in your marketing plan to attract new customers?

_____

_____

_____

_____

_____

10. If 70 percent of a buying decision happens in-store, what are you doing to ensure that decision is a positive one?

_____

_____

_____

_____

11. Do your visual merchandising efforts contribute to your bottomline? How would you rate your visual merchandising on a scale of one to 10? What can you do to make it a 10?

12. What products and services do customers really buy from you? How do you communicate your benefits?

13. Where have you searched in the past month for marketing inspiration, innovative marketing ideas?

14. What new solutions can you incorporate into your marketing strategy today? What new solutions can you begin to develop for the future?

15. How are you "tangibilizing" your intangibles and "intangibilizing" your tangibles?

16. What have you achieved in the last year, last month, last week to stay ahead of copycats? Is your marketing strategy putting you on the offensive or defensive?

17. How are you using emerging technology to update your marketing strategy and its benefits?

18. What is your best selling item? How often is it out-of-stock? What is your most requested service? How difficult is it for customers to get?

19. How many new items/services have you added to your merchandising plan this year? How much will they contribute in gross margin dollars?

_____

_____

_____

_____

_____

20. What dilemma must merchandising create for your customers?

_____

_____

_____

_____

_____

21. Is there still opening night excitement in your business? If not, what are you doing to revive that feeling?

_____

_____

_____

_____

_____

Write in one additional question you feel is important to you, your situation as a result of reading this section — *and then answer it.*

Q. _____

_____

_____

_____

_____

_____

_____

A. _____

_____

_____

_____

_____

_____

_____

_____

_____

_____

MERCHANDISING ADDENDUM

A discussion of marketing wouldn't be complete without a word or two about the merchandise chosen for sale. Although my word or two is focused toward the retailer, it is by no means exclusive to this community, since the lessons are applicable to every marketer.

PARETO'S PRINCIPLE
20 percent of your
customers (or products)
account for 80 percent
of your sales.

Vilfredo Pareto (1848-1923)
Philosopher and mathematician

20/80 MERCHANDISING

In merchandising your store do you use the 20/80 principle of core marketing? Do you know what the 20/80 principle is? Many merchants don't. That's why at season's end, you see piles of inventory at 50, 60, 70 percent off. My mother-in-law recently purchased an end-of-season coat for 70 percent off. The discount kept getting greater each time she went to the store. Had she waited another week or so, the store probably would have paid her to take it. Understanding and using the 20/80 principle is the start of effective inventory management. It's managing your "core business"—*the reason you are there.*

In today's business climate, we are well aware that effective management is the determinant for survival. We look at our business dollars and smile: profits! profits! profits! But consider that out of every business dollar approximately 50 cents goes toward cost of goods, about another 20 cents for staff, yet another 25 cents for the cost of doing business, the rent, the fixtures, the common area.

Out of the 5 cents left *(our profit)* is the cost of lost merchandise and markdowns. Our margin for profit is small—*very small indeed.* When we fritter away even one cent of our dollar, we can easily slip from black to red. Nowhere is effective management more essential than where it meets inventory planning and control. It is here that your dollars spent and your profits earned are most visible—laudatory or condemning.

To effect change, to stay ahead of the competition, your dollars spent, your profits earned, your inventory performance must be constantly evaluated and improved.

One of the most effective methods to evaluate performance is through a comprehensive inventory planning and development program—one that is an integral component of

A competitive world has two possibilities for you. You can lose. Or, if you want to win, you can change.

Lester C. Thurow, Dean
Sloan School of Management, M.I.T.
60 Minutes, CBS TV

your strategic planning *(not a casual, as it happens component).* The following information provides an excellent perspective with which to evaluate and improve your inventory productivity and hence your bottomline profitability.

Studies have shown that 80 percent of your inventory *(or of the services you provide)* gives you only 20 percent of your revenue. This being the case, 20 percent of your inventory *(or services you provide),* therefore gives you 80 percent of your revenue.

It stands to reason if some of that important 20 percent of your inventory is out of stock, is in poor condition, is stale, you lose a disproportionate number of sales. *(In fact, at least four times the loss that you would incur were you out of stock of some of the other 80 percent of your inventory).*

> *Selling: getting rid of stuff.*
> *Marketing: having the*
> *stuff to get rid of.*
> Sam Geist

What is your best item? Is it "your best selling" item or "your best-return-on-investment" item? Effective inventory management depends on your answer. Profit and loss depend on your answer.

GMROI

GMROI *(Gross Margin Return on Investment)* was developed to assist marketers make these vital merchandising calculations profitably. It is a management planning and decision making tool that identifies and evaluates whether an adequate gross margin is being earned by your products or services, compared to the investment in inventory or time, required to generate those gross margin dollars.

It is the engine that spurs action, keeps business focused on its core, identifies profitability. It is one of the most effective methods to evaluate—improve— control inventory.

GMROI assists to change the business focus from sales to profitability, from percentages to dollars. During one of my earliest **GMROI** merchandising sessions, I asked one of the buyers in the audience what her division contributed to the company as a whole. Her response, "42 percent," encouraged me to change the title of my program to "You Pay Bills With Dollars...Not Percentages." I asked her, **"When was the last time you took 42 percent to the bank?"**

GMROI identifies and differentiates paper profits, which seem to be much easier to produce from realized profits, which is what you take to the bank.

As one of the most effective methods to evaluate, improve and control inventory, **GMROI** assists you to understand the business of profits versus return on investment.

The benefits of **GMROI**:

1. *It reveals where actual dollar profits versus paper profits are attained in the merchandise plan.*

2. *It focuses the merchandiser's attention on return on investment as a basis for merchandising decisions.*

3. *It focuses the merchandiser's attention on SKUs (stock keeping units) rather than department totals.*

4. *It improves merchandising decisions, including the visual merchandising plan.*

5. *It identifies product "winners" and those products "starving to become winners."*

6. *It identifies lazy assets — redundant stock.*

7. *It frees up inventory cash for product re-investment.*

8. *It identifies "core" business/never outs.*

9. *It drops more dollars to the bottom line.*

10. *It unites buyer performance and compensation.*

GMROI is, of course, not the only factor to be considered in making merchandising decisions. Cost of sales, overhead, customer preferences also play an important role. However the objective value of **GMROI** should not be minimized.

The basic GMROI formula.

GM %	X	Sales at Retail	=	GMROI
(Gross Margin)		Average Inventory in $ @ cost		(Gross Margin Return on Investment)

To find **GMROI,** follow these four steps:

STEP ONE

Calculate your gross margin or realized gross margin as a percentage.

Formula for calculating gross margin (GM):

Sales - cost of goods sold

Example:

Sales =	$1,000,000
Cost of goods =	520,000
Gross Margin (GM) =	$480,000

To calculate GM as a percentage, divide GM by your total sales.

Example: 480,000 ÷ 1,000,000 = .48 or 48 percent

STEP TWO

Calculate your average inventory at cost.

Formula to calculate your inventory at cost:

Add up your remaining inventory for every month plus the
remaining inventory from the previous year.
Divide the total by 13 (the number of inventories listed).

Example:

Sum of all inventory = $2,600,000

Divide ÷ by 13

Average inventory at cost = $200,000

STEP THREE

**Divide your total sales by your average inventory at cost.
This will give you your ratio of sales to inventory investment.**

Formula to calculate your sales-to-inventory investment ratio:

Divide total sales by average inventory at cost.

Example:

Total Sales = $1,000,000

Average inventory at cost =   200,000

Sales-to-inventory investment ratio =   5

Note: This is not your inventory turnover rate.

STEP FOUR

Multiply the result of Step Three by your gross margin percentage to get GMROI.

Formula to calculate **GMROI** percentage:

Multiply gross margin (GM) percentage by sales-to-investment ratio.

Example: GMROI = 48 percent x 5 = 240 percent

Your **GMROI** *(Gross Margin Return on Investment)* for all goods in this example is 240 percent or $2.40 for every dollar of merchandise investment.

Once you have completed this exercise, you can repeat it, to determine how each department fares against your store **GMROI** average.

The beauty of this concept is that it works for any size store, department or merchandise classification. That is, it works for each category of each department, each class in each category, each color, each size in each class and so on.

You can also compare your **GMROI** to your competitors to see how well you are doing from an industry standpoint.

Keeping a close watch on your **GMROI** results will enable you to ensure that your inventory works as hard for your business as you do.

USE THE GMROI FORMULA ON YOUR SKUS

Calculate your gross margin or realized gross margin as a percentage.

Sales - cost of goods sold

Calculate your average inventory at cost.

Divide the total remaining inventory by 13

Divide your total sales by your average inventory at cost.

This will give you your ratio of sales to inventory investment.

Multiply the result by your gross margin percentage to get GMROI.

Multiply gross margin (GM) percentage by sales-to-investment ratio.

Part four highlights the strategies to provide "heroic" service every day from the customer's perspective. Customer needs and wants are discussed, including effective dialoguing — long term relationship building — customerized service — added value and customer comfort. The section concludes with 15 suggestions for instituting a service plan that answers *"Why should someone do business with you... rather than someone else?"*

Execution is the Service Strategy

4

How do you "do" customer service?

How does your staff "do" customer service?

How do your customers expect customer service to be done?

Is there any correlation between your actions, your service execution and your customers' expectations?

I have experienced "service" across the continent by many, many service providers and can unequivocally say, *we still don't get it!*

We don't seem to remember that *serve* is in the word service, that the dictionary definition for service is: *performance of labor for the benefit of another; the act of serving; a helpful act.*

We don't seem to remember that research shows huge numbers of customers are lost because of staff indifference.

Out of frustration with the sorry state of affairs, I changed the title of the customer service program I regularly present,

> *Customer Service Secret #1 is to treat customers like your life depends on it, because it does.*
>
> Sam Geist

from C.A.R.E. (Customers Are Really Everything) to "If I Hear Customer Service One More Time, I'll...."

It's time to stop talking about service and start providing solutions. Become a solution provider.

HEROIC CUSTOMER SERVICE

CBC News related that in Kelowna, British Columbia, the delivery man for a local take-out pizzeria, was held up, the robbers demanding he hand over all his money. He did. They drove away. He delivered all his pizzas before they got cold and then phoned the police. That delivery driver is a hero. His pizzeria basks in his glory.

Who defines this heroic act? What message does it send? As I see it, it demonstrates an uncompromising regard for the customer.

That's what exemplary service is: uncompromising, unconditional customer regard.

It starts with personalizing each customer, making them more than just an invoice number or identification number or account number. In our impersonal, voice-messaged, computerized world, customers, more than ever, want to be thought of as real people.

Service can be viewed from a *share-of-customer perspective* rather than a *market share perspective*. Using this perspective, the focus is on using service to get the biggest share of each individual customer. It is based on getting each customer to buy more and/or buy more often, rather than concentrating primarily on getting more customers. Demonstrating customer service in this strategy goes like this:

Last year a friend of mine ordered flowers for his mom's birthday from a florist in the small town where he lives. The florist delivered as expected and my friend and his mom were satisfied.

This year, two weeks before his mom's birthday *(that is, two weeks before the date of last year's order)*, my friend got a note from this florist: "Your mom's birthday is coming up! Last year we sent her freesias and spider mums, what would you like to do this year? We recommend a glass bowl of tiny roses."

In a corporate environment, demonstrating customer service to enlarge the share of your customers' spending might go like this:

I ordered an iron and ironing board sent to my room when I checked in at the Ritz-Carlton Hotel in Los Angeles, California. When I check in at the Ritz-Carlton Hotel in Naples, Florida they'll ask if I'd like an iron and ironing board sent up. The hotel uses the Covia airline reservation system and has recorded more than 400,000 individual customer preferences.

Both the local florist and the hotel are using information technology to provide exemplary customer service. Both are using common sense to satisfy and gain a larger share of their customers' spending.

BE WHAT YOU SAY

Make the commitment. It is a tremendous competitive advantage. At its most fundamental, providing this exemplary level of service, being what you say, requires fulfilling these basic precepts:

1. *Be Prepared — Know Your Customers.*

2. *Get Close to Customers by Dialoguing.*

3. *Focus on Maintaining a Long Term Relationship.*

4. *Customer-ize Your Service.*

5. *Deliver "Value."*

6. *Ensure Customer Comfort.*

7. *Benchmark Yourself.*

8. *Take Care of the Details.*

9. *Create Heroic Service Givers.*

10. *Institute A Service Action Plan.*

In the end, it's quite simple: *"be"* what you say!!

BE PREPARED

Begin with research. Read. Ask. Question. Discuss. Distribute questionnaires. Make phone calls. Talk to customers, to staff, to friends. Make notes. Strategize. Implement. Research. Read. Ask....

The cycle never stops, because your

Talk does not cook rice.

Chinese Proverb

customers' expectations, interests, desires and needs are not static. *"To be"* most effectively, use a checklist faithfully. You would be quite uncomfortable, if just before take-off you found out that on your particular flight, the pilots decided not to carry out their customary pre-flight check, which they always conducted to make certain nothing had been overlooked in their preparations. They decided that this particular run didn't warrant preparing themselves, the crew, the plane. They've flown before. They know what to do. They are just going to take off.

Your run, your mission to provide exemplary customer service, is no less important an assignment.

Prepare and use your personal checklist. Include everything that affects your customer service:

- out of stock merchandise
- damaged products
- pricing
- delivery routes
- late arrivals
- follow-up
- signing
- product knowledge

- housekeeping
- packaging
- computer maintenance
- phone lines
- performance
- staff training
- hours of operation
- new merchandise

Ask senior staff/frontline staff to do a "walk through" regularly, notebook in hand. Their observations should be incorporated into the checklist, which will evolve, reflecting new concerns. Customers are not disappointed. Their expectations are not only met, *they are exceeded* — the hazards of overpromising and underdelivering are eliminated.

Checklists provide a must-ensure-it-happens focus. They ease the planning process, the development, the administration and follow-up to special promotions, events and projects. Not only are they valuable in everyday business life, they are vital in the business environments of manufacturers, service agencies, retailers, catalog houses and professional services. Checklists draw attention to the simple "must do" details like promotional signs on displays. They remind about cross-promotional merchandising opportunities *(possibilities often missed without a checklist)*. Checklists highlight prospects to call, customers to follow-up with, resources and suppliers to contact. They also jog the memory for more important details, such as the timely arrival of promotional merchandise, correct pricing, bonus options, delivery deadlines and special instructions. *You are able to underpromise and overdeliver!*

Whether it's to promote change, encourage innovation, or control the myriad of everyday business life details, "a living checklist" assists you take excellent care of business by taking exemplary care of your customers.

Portraying Steven Seagal's archenemy in Under Siege II, Eric Bogosian reiterated the advantages of a checklist with his terse line, "Chance favors the prepared mind." It does indeed.

Jan Carlson, President and CEO of Scandinavian Airlines System, coined a phrase about preparing staff that should be part of the lexicon of every business. His "moments of truth" allude to each point of contact between your company and your customers. These occasions offer opportunity to serve or disserve. They hold the potential to build, maintain or destroy the relationship.

There are countless "moments of truth" in your organization, involving your staff — from the receptionist — to the delivery man — to the warehouse manager — to the phone operator — to the maintenance man — to the reservations attendant — to the.... Find them and make them shining moments of triumph — memorable moments of unparalleled customer service, "moments of truth."

> *The people answering the phones (at businesses across America) are a major competitive asset— or liability.*
>
> Tom Peters, business writer
> *USA Today*

GET CLOSE TO CUSTOMERS BY DIALOGUING

An effective service strategy strongly depends on honest, upfront dialogue. Such dialogue ensures the quality customer feedback that you need to keep on improving. Three requirements for win/win dialogue include:

- *Being able and willing to communicate (trust!).*

- *Getting/giving rewards for participation (keep WIFM in mind).*

- *Participating in dialogue that results in behavior change for everyone involved.*

Once these criteria are met, getting close to customers becomes much easier.

- *Dialogue with them.*

- *Collect and assess their feedback.*

- *Check often that everyone is on the same wavelength.*

- *Check that the information you gather from customers is in sync with your interpretation and perception of the situation.*

Very often, too often, we assume. We misunderstand. We see what we hope to see, what we want to see, what we're prepared to see rather than what is really there.

Some interesting findings came to light when the Gallup Organization for the Quality Research Institute conducted a survey on how well retailers and their customers knew each other.

- As they continued to work to improve service at their discount retail outlets, 61 percent of executives interviewed thought their service had indeed improved over the past year. However, only 30 percent of their customers noticed any improvement.

- When questioned about the quality of their merchandise, 33 percent of interviewed executives believed it exceeded the expectations of their customers, while only 18 percent of shoppers expressed the same sentiments.

- Some 70 percent of executives felt their products, in general, were of good value. A disappointing 24 percent of customers concurred.

- Focusing on speedy service, half the executives questioned were certain their "speedy" service exceeded customer expectations. Only 17 percent of customers agreed.

It doesn't take much to conclude that these retailers and their customers were not seeing eye to eye at all. The implications of this situation are disturbing. **How effective can evolving strategies be when they are based on erroneous assumptions instead of accurate information? How can you convince customers to do business with you? How can you possibly overdeliver if you misunderstand?**

Dialoguing is talking *(asking lots of questions)* AND *(mostly)* listening. Stay close to customers by listening carefully to what they have to say. They will tell you what they want: the products and services they are willing to pay for.

In 1984 GM decided that its Cadillac was too long and shrunk it. Sales shrunk too. Did anyone ask customers what they wanted?

When GM finally decided that dialoguing, that getting feedback made sense, they discovered some interesting facts. Customers had their own ideas about what they wanted in a car. GM gave them the opportunity to assist with the new design. The results? A new DeVille and Fleetwood. Sales? Up 36 percent from the previous year.

John Fleming, Cadillac's General Director of Marketing & Product Planning recognized the vital role customers play *(to buy or not to buy)*. "A very tough lesson. We learned to pay great attention to the customer."

Spend time regularly with customers, listening—not selling. Listening is not a public relations ploy. It is realizing that there is a great deal to be learned from customers. They have become better and better informed, have more and more options and are more and more demanding. Believe it!

Luciano Benetton, the world-renowned Italian textile merchant, recognized how vital listening to customers was to his success.

Customers are your business. Know what they're thinking. Know what they want. Satisfy them.

Customers are a finite commodity. They are not like buses, another one coming along

---

Listen. Don't explain or justify.

William G. Dyer
Brigham Young University
Strategies for Managing Change

I must get out into the world where I can sense the preferences of people, see what they like.... I can talk to people who teach me about their markets.

Luciano Benetton
Benetton Group SPA

in 20 minutes. Research has illustrated again and again that keeping one of your customers is *one fifth the cost of finding a new customer.* Hold on to them. Get close — stay close by putting them first. Everyone wants to be numero uno. Make them feel important. They are!

FOCUS ON MAINTAINING A LONG-TERM RELATIONSHIP

Build and sustain an enviable relationship with your customers by utilizing the same strategies that would assist you to maintain an excellent relationship in your private life. Keeping customers for the long term by satisfying them offers major rewards — rewards that are translated to bottomline profitability.

Mail-order company, Lands' End considers maintaining a long-term relationship by improving customer service a business mandate. Most of its $21 million in capital expenditures over a two year period in the late 1980s was earmarked toward service improvement. Techno updating included new equipment to hem pants faster as well as new sorting and packaging equipment to get merchandise to customers faster.

Customers have come to trust Lands' End. They believe they

As the world becomes more and more competitive, you have to sharpen all your tools. Knowing what's on the customer's mind is the most important thing we can do.

Richard E. Heckert, former Chairman
DuPont
Fortune

There is only one boss — the customer. And he can fire everybody in the company from the chairman on down, simply by spending his money somewhere else.

Sam Walton, founder
Wal-Mart

can tell Lands' End what they feel, what they want, and Lands' End will respond. *And they do,* further solidifying the relationship, creating and sustaining customer loyalty!

A Small Aside. The bikes used to be delivered three days later, but the company stopped the quick turn-around when it realized customers didn't believe that a quality, customized vehicle could be built so quickly.

Other companies use slightly different but no less effective strategies to keep customers close. In Kokubu, Japan, the National Bicycle Industrial Company custom-makes bikes to the specifications of new owners. Customers are measured and custom fitted. They are able to choose the handlebars they want, the tires, seat, color, up to 11,231,862 variations on its models and have it delivered two weeks later.

CUSTOMER-IZE YOUR SERVICE

Car manufacturers are now pledging a much higher degree of "customer-ization" thanks to innovative computer technology. New cars are heavily computerized to learn drivers' habits: how you accelerate, brake, take corners. The car is then able to anticipate the way you drive, thereby saving fuel. It recognizes you, *the driver,* by weight. It then adjusts the seat, the air conditioning, heat, and so on, to your preferences. The computer learning process takes about two months, and at the end of that time you own a "customer-ized" car. When it's time for a new purchase, **do you choose another make of car and re-teach it all that it has learned, or do you use the existing data and inject the computerized information chip into your next purchase?**

Blockbuster Entertainment is piloting the installation of in-store computer kiosks so customers can come up with their own Top Ten movie list. The computer-kiosks integrate information regarding what customers have already seen with the types of films they would enjoy renting. Using a touch screen, customers choose from the compatible list and check availability as well. Preferences are updated regularly. Video renting as hassle free as it gets.

Develop and institute a plan that holds as its basic premise that markets are made up of single customers with individual needs and wants. Such a plan is "customer-ized" and personalized to a market of one, demonstrating your understanding that business grows one dollar at a time — one sale at a time — one customer at a time. Customers are happy. They remain in the relationship, since finding a new relationship as beneficial elsewhere necessitates teaching their new partner their likes, dislikes, wants and needs. *Staying close — really close to customers is the secret weapon to customer retention.*

Other companies enhance their service by aligning themselves with respected, globally recognized partners. In this way, resources are pooled, marketing strategies are consolidated, growth is maximized, quality is prioritized, and in the process, a global perspective of customer service is incorporated. Communication companies like British Telecom and MCI did it *(and are merging in the process)*. Airlines such as KLM and Northwest are doing it. Fast food outlets, like McDonald's, and its supplier, Coca-Cola are doing it. The result? The often intangible, fragile tentacles of customer service stretch to the four corners of the globe — far beyond the reach of the brand name alone.

> *We set the price.*
> *The customer sets the value.*
>
> Sam Geist

McDonald's provides an outstanding example of an organization that operates with a single-minded, obsessive devotion to institutionalized organizational refinement. Simply put: they ensure that change is controlled, continuous and very focused. The customer perspective is always, but always at the forefront of its action plan.

A couple of quick McXamples.

Although they received no pressure from customers, McDonald's U.S. management saw the writing on the wall and banned all cigarette smoking from U.S. company-owned restaurants. They encouraged franchisees to do the same. Tobacco companies were upset, visibly shaken by McDonald's "no smoking" policy and requested the opportunity to discuss the decision. McDonald's refused. It took a stand in the interest of its customers — and stuck with it.

Beef! A McDonald's mainstay. Charges that beef purchased for burgers was obtained from cattle grazing on pastures created by clearing rain forests was quickly and emphatically denied. Beef! A McDonald's mainstay. In the midst of Britain's furor over mad cow disease, British beef was quickly removed from British locations and replaced with imported beef.

McDonald's understands that customers are everything. Customers are the judge, jury and executioner. There are no pardons. There are no stays of execution. Customers must be satisfied, must feel confident, must feel trust in the relationship *(that's absolutely at the core)* or they go elsewhere.

Their staunch service stance begs a question or two — **what do *your* customers want? Do you know? Do you provide it?**

What does customer service mean to your customers? Is there anything else you can do to satisfy your customers that you aren't already doing?

The ability to identify your customers' service expectations, meet them, and hopefully go on to exceed them, within your environment, offers you a tremendous competitive advantage.

We believe many hotels get too distracted by advertising, promotions, and giveaways and lose sight of the basics. The only real way to differentiate yourself from the competition is through service.

For instance, we believe in guest recognition rather than guest rewards. What's more, we've found that our guests prefer it that way. They prefer to be upgraded to a suite, to be remembered by name, and to receive their favorite amenity, rather than pay a higher room rate so that we can afford to send them on a free trip to Europe.

Jonathan Tisch, President
Loews Hotels
Successful Meetings

Jeffrey Mount, president of Wright's Gourmet House in Tampa realizes exactly what customers want and why they come to his restaurant for it.

"In my restaurant, it's not ham-and-cheese sandwiches we're selling. It may look like ham and cheese. It may taste like ham

and cheese. But it's not a ham and cheese sandwich. It's a good time. People spend their money with businesses that make them feel good. It's as simple as that. We try to make our customers feel good."

DELIVER VALUE

Customers expect "value."

Value as an equation, states:
Product + Quality + Price
+ Service = Value
Each customer decides
how much importance
to attach to each element.

Sam Geist

A survey conducted by the U.S. Home Improvement Center's Customer Panel asked customers to define "good value." Their list included:

- *products guaranteed to work, to last*

- *well-built equipment, with no hidden defects*

- *a money-back guarantee*

- *a warranty*

- *quality products at low affordable prices*

- *products that look good, solve a problem, are easy to use, come with good instructions.*

Exemplary customer service is good value. It is incorporated through your assurance of replacement or money-back guarantee. It is incorporated through your convenient operations, your speedy service. It is incorporated through your expertise, through your trained, reliable, informative staff. Good service is incorporated through your promise of quality, your well-made products, your efficient, competent services, your truthful claims and fulfilled expectations.

Give your products, your services, added perceived value by creating a "benefit- oriented" environment. Michael Pierce, owner of the year round Christmas store, Christmas By the Sea, realizes the importance of creating a benefit orientation. He recognizes that selling Christmas baubles as tree ornaments in July just doesn't quite do it. However by positioning his products with the additional aura of *"memories of Christmas wished for, never had, but can now afford,"* or as *"promises to children of Christmases yet to come,"* the elaborate ornaments take on a mantle of perceived added value, closing the gap between browsers and buyers.

Offer added value by considering your busy customers' availability of time — *or lack of it*. Today, with time considered a "value" commodity, be as considerate with their time as you would be with their wallets.

Research has shown that the longer you ask customers to wait to complete their purchase, the less likely they will be to buy. The accounting firm, Ernst & Young, in its 1994 survey for

---

YOUR CUSTOMERS' VIEW OF GOOD VALUE

I have some tools and equipment 20 to 30 years old that are as good today as when I bought them–that's good value.

A.E. Perras

A decent price, a decent warranty, and no-problem, no-questions-asked replacement.

G. Belt

Functional, unique and irresistibly priced.

L. Lee

Good product, good price, good warranty, good service and advice is good value.

R. Jones

Home Improvement Center

Macy's Department Store in New York City, found that in 23 percent of the situations where customers were required to wait a long time to complete their purchase, they either postponed or canceled it. The problem seems to be two-fold. Many of today's customers really are busy and can't afford to waste their time. In addition to "time poverty," customers feel they are not considered important when they're asked to wait. Customers holding "high-ticket" items feel neglected and angry at having to wait while customers with less costly items are checked through. And customers, who have small purchases, have second thoughts about standing in line with something "minor."

"Time" is often an issue in regard to "big-ticket" purchases that must be delivered and assembled. Selling big-ticket items such as furniture and appliances and then requiring customers to wait an inappropriately long time for delivery or asking them to pay for assembly, does nothing to encourage customers to associate you or your business with value.

Customers who feel neglected, frustrated, occasionally exhibit their exasperation in unusual ways. Getting off the escalator on the second floor of the Bay, a department store with locations across Canada, I saw a woman cup her hands around her mouth, megaphone style, and holler at the top of her lungs, "Is there anyone who works for the Bay up here on the second floor?" She could not have expressed her feelings of discouragement more clearly.

Hold onto the realization and strategies that clearly exemplify that "value" is defined by your customers, *the recipients,* not by you, *the provider.*

Give customers a greater perception of the value of your products with bonus sizes, two-for-ones, multi-packs, complementary products packed together. Give them a greater perception of value with new, improved features, continuous quality improvement, better, more efficient service.

> *To create business requires knowing what customers think quality is. This precedes all else in business.*
>
> Theodore Levitt, editor and writer
> *Harvard Business Review*

But most important, give them added value with exemplary customer service. It provides an outstanding means of differentiation.

Hire staff who make a difference, who add value by their expertise, their services, their demeanor.

My son Aaron, weary after working at his job all summer long, was anxious to visit friends in England before university resumed. Wanting to help him out financially, I offered to get him a flight ticket using my accumulated air mile points. As luck would have it *(for him),* the only "point" seats available were for business class. We arrived at the airport, Aaron in jeans, backpack slung across his back, dragging his huge duffel bag, only to be greeted by a long, long British Airways check-in line. An airline attendant, directing traffic, gave Aaron a quick look-over and pointed condescendingly to the end of the economy-class line.

Walking up behind him, I reminded Aaron he was flying business class and indicated *that* check-in counter. The attendant hurried over to us. Surveyed Aaron's ticket. Removed his mask of condescension and with newfound, smiling enthusiasm said, "Right this way, sir! Let me take your bag, sir!" as he grabbed Aaron's duffel and pulled it over to the counter, explaining all the while about the amenities of business class in London.

We still smile about this incident. You just can't judge a customer by his jeans or the luggage he carries.

Become an organization that operates from a value-added perspective, incorporating your products, your services, your employees, so your entire organization becomes bigger than the individual departments, staff or products.

At the Hyatt Regency Chicago, Jim Evans, Senior VP of Sales and Marketing is just one of Hyatt's top executives who become waiters, bell hops, door men during Hyatt In Touch Day so they can easily see and solve the needs of their customers. Staff are encouraged to report discoveries they have made that will improve their guests' experience at the hotel.

TD Bank's, Greenline investor services, in Canada, uses Datapac, a private secured network to offer their customers access to their accounts from anywhere in Canada. Bank of Montreal's new mbanx offers full service banking by phone, fax, automated bank machine or on-line

When you add value to service:
1 + 1 = 3
Sam Geist

any time and rewards users with cash rewards.

Look out for opportunities to add value and capitalize on the rich benefits offering it can give. A friend of mine required a non-standard size pool cover for his unusually shaped swimming hole. To him value-added is the supplier who offers flexibility and speed in providing the needed cover.

At the first supplier, he is told that their covers are all standard sizes..."never changed them, never will...and what you want is just too expensive. Use two standard covers, sewn together."

At the second supplier he is told that they understand his request. They think that they can supply the cover as requested but will double check with their cover manufacturer first. Finally they asked when the cover was required. The second supplier added value in several ways. His helpful attitude indicated value-added. His behavior *(ready and willing to be flexible)* indicated value-added. His follow-up *(a commitment to check out probability with his man-ufacturer)* and his interest *(fixing in his mind, when the cover will be required so he can get the wheels in motion as required)* indicated a value-added approach.

From my friend's perspective, there's no contest who will be his supplier of choice again and again and again. Value-added decided that.

When all is said and done, staying close to your customers must be the starting point for everything you do. Only by staying close can you "see value" through your customers' eyes, offer value-added,

> *I have the simplest of taste.*
> *I'm easily satisfied with the best.*
>
> Oscar Wilde, (1854-1900),
> Irish poet, playwright and novelist

and provide the quality service that puts you in one-of-a-kind company.

Paul Grimes, editor-at-large for Travelers Condé Nast magazine travels the globe searching for value for his readers. While he readily acknowledges that the evidence of luxury varies according to the star-rating of the establishment *(hotel or restaurant)*, the value for its price, the evidence of customer service should not be compromised. Travelers may not expect as much from a two star establishment as they do from a four star, but regardless of its cost, they want the level of value, of service that creates a satisfying, comfortable experience.

As a frequent traveler myself, I can certainly agree. Very often the value that is added to "the bed" costs the hotel little, but greatly increases the comfort, the enjoyment and finally the quality of the experience. A wake-up call, given twice to ensure that you did indeed get moving, an iron and ironing board, a coffee machine and supplies, a newspaper, the promise that if you forgot your toothpaste, it will actually be supplied, a quick check out. It's all the little things, the details that add value.

While speaking in Orlando, Florida I stayed the night at the Villas of Grand Cypress, where the bathmats were like the ones at home, the bars of soap were full size, the towels were colored. I felt comfortable, relaxed, at home. It's all the little things, the details that echo customer consideration long after the experience is over.

I remember having extensive carpentry done at our house on two separate occasions. The first time the workers left in their wake shavings, wood chips and mess every night. My wife ran around vacuuming, cleaning up after them, tears in her eyes and choice words on her breath, knowing that the next evening and every evening until they finished, a repetition of her task would be required.

The second time we hired someone who added value by putting down drop sheets wherever he worked, vacuuming up each day's shavings before he left — and doing a professional carpentry job to boot. His respect of our home was remembered and appreciated long after the carpentry was completed. He certainly carried his "checklist" with him — and used it.

Add value by partnering. It can provide a greater range of services such as vendor managed inventory, just-in-time delivery, specialty services, training, technological innovations, buying syndicates — all are services that benefit your customer.

ENSURE CUSTOMER COMFORT

Customers not only have deeply rooted "value" expectations, they also hold firmly established "inner values" that validate and

> *I once heard someone describe value-added this way: "Imagine your biggest customer walking into your office, sitting down, and asking you to tell him how he benefits from you being there. If you can answer to his satisfaction, then you're probably a value-added employee."*
> *It's a good test that everyone should pass.*
>
> Dave Radin, communications manager
> Corning Consumer Products
> *DM News*

reinforce their own identity. It is for this very reason that customers shop in stores that re-affirm their image of themselves, and they do business with people with whom they have an affinity.

How customers perceive your company, influences their decision to buy. **Do you connect with your customers? Does your business environment reflect your customers comfort level or are they uncomfortable and anxious to leave? Are you underwhelming them with too little choice, or overwhelming them with too much choice, thereby diminishing their own sense of capability?**

It *is* true. There is an optimum level of available choice when you are dealing with customers' inner values and needs. Not enough choice leaves customers feeling a lack of value, while excessive choice leaves them uncomfortable, confused, over-whelmed, unable to decide. It is your job to guide your customers toward a decision. Especially in areas of highly interchangeable products or services, the need to assist customers with problematic choices of similar offerings becomes all the more important.

When my daughter decided to attend university in Chicago, we contacted a real estate agent to show us apartments. Before he opened his listing book, he asked Rebecca a number of questions: Where was she attending school? What was her schedule like? Did she have a car? Did she have friends in Chicago? What recreational activities did she enjoy? What features would she like? Did she have a preferred location? Price range? and on and on. He listened to her answers. Finally he checked his listings and described four apartments he felt were appropriate. We were disappointed. We wanted more choice. He was quite firm, telling us more would only confuse us. Once we'd discussed what we saw, we could look further he said. He was absolutely right! He had synthesized Rebecca's requirements with his availability so well that we were able to make a decision by the time we saw the fourth apartment.

Everyone enjoys the latest, the newest, the most exciting. Keep your customers comfortable, satisfied, by providing a high level of innovation.

3M incorporates this customer need for "new" as part of its commitment to its customers' comfort and satisfaction. The company goal is that 25 percent of its business each year must come from products and services that are less than five years old — recent innovations. This goal forces 3M to position itself on the leading edge — a position its customers appreciate.

Find out and incorporate into your strategic plans what your customers value. Create new opportunities based on your customers' needs — their physical needs, their emotional needs. Such a strategy insures success. It also presents an irony that must be recognized and addressed.

> *We're in the process of downsizing and are using the "value-added yardstick" to determine which jobs should remain and which jobs are not necessary because they do not add value to the product.*
>
> Anonymous, A Major Manufacturing Company
> *DM News*

Most likely, if you are successful at staying close to your customers, your business will grow. Growth necessitates by its very nature incorporating *new ways to get and stay close to customers*. The strategies used when you were small may now be inappropriate. Organizational restructuring may be necessary. Maintaining a flexible, always-learning, always-changing internal environment makes restructuring much less painful.

BENCHMARK YOURSELF

Be tough on yourself. Benchmark against yourself. Measure your service achievements against achievements of last year, last month, last week.

Benchmark yourself against your competitors. Call on your competitors as a customer and determine your satisfaction of their competencies. Call your own organization and again check your satisfaction.

Ascertain levels of efficiency, accuracy, courtesy and assistance at your competitors and also in your own organization. Keep track. Focus on improvement.

L.L. Bean, the U.S. mail-order giant, stays a healthy giant by measuring every aspect of its customers' experiences carefully. It tracks its own performance in seven critical areas. It rates. It investigates. It asks. It works to improve:

- **Convenience:** *How long does a customer have to wait until an operator picks up the phone?*

  - *85-90 percent of calls must be answered within three rings.*
  - *more than two percent of abandoned calls is not acceptable.*

- **Product Guarantee:** *This area reflects on the quality — and the customer satisfaction.*

- **In-stock Availability:** *Can't sell what isn't available.*

  - *How long does it take for customers to figure out that if you haven't got it, there's little point in including you on their shopping list?*

- **Fulfillment Time:** *Customers may have a change of heart if they're required to wait too long.*

- **Innovation:** *Introduce new products and procedures*

- **Image:** *Does it continue to reflect your customers' image positively? Does it make customers feel good about themselves? Feel comfortable?*

- **Retail Service:** *How well is the mail order service translated in the retail environment?*

L.L. Bean benchmarks against itself. It also benchmarks against its competitors.

Worthy of Note:

Customers have done their own checking and made their own

comparisons of mail-order houses against retail operators. They have cast their vote in favor of the mail order houses by conducting their business with them.

Their decision represented a huge volume in credit card purchases over the 1995 Christmas season in the United States:

- *Mail-order VISA charges were up 19.6 percent to $2.12 billion.*

- *Department store VISA charges were $1.6 billion.*

- *Discounters VISA charges were $1 billion .*

This is why according to *USA Today*, December 1995:

- *Mail-order houses offer time savings.*

- *Their advertising is straightforward.*

- *Service is good. Phone representatives know what they're talking about. They're not just order takers.*

- *Mail order houses don't offer confusing discounts. Pricing is clear.*

TAKE CARE OF DETAILS

It is the responsibility of management to ensure that the entire organization is involved in customer service, by monitoring customers' needs. It is management's responsibility to clarify not only the do's and the don'ts but also the *why's and wherefore's*.

Ernst & Young 1994 research found that price *(too expensive)* was a deterrent to purchase in only about 8 percent of "no-sale" situations. The larger *(much larger)* reasons for a "no sale" are environment related reasons such as appearance and conduct of staff, perceived honesty of business, refund and return policies, reputation of integrity and atmosphere.

Even more serious than loss of sale, is loss of customer. A study conducted by the American Society of Quality Control has shown that 68 percent of customer attrition is caused by staff indifference, while only one customer in seven divorces a business because of product dissatisfaction.

Customers lost because of indifference are very difficult, if not impossible, to regain.

This anonymous little poem says it all.

> *There's no magic formula for staying close to your customer. It's basic consideration, time, effort, commitment and follow-up.*
>
> Stanley C. Gault, Chairman & CEO
> Goodyear Tire & Rubber Company

Remember Me!

*I'm the fellow who goes into
a restaurant, sits down and patiently
waits while the waitresses finish
their visiting before taking my order.*

*I'm the fellow who goes into a
department store and stands quietly
while the clerks chit chat.*

*I'm the fellow who drives into a
service station and never blows
his horn, but lets the attendant
take his time.*

*You might say, I'm the good guy.
Do you know who else I am?
I'm the fellow who never comes back.*

*It amuses me to see business
spending so much money every year
to get me back when I was there
in the first place!*

*All they needed to do was give me
some service and extend a little courtesy.*

*In fact, I was the most important
person in the world to them.*

I WAS A CUSTOMER!

Develop a forum for open-minded listening so no matter whether you are in mail-order, in manufacturing, in service or in retail, you know the answers to ***"Why should someone do business with you...rather than someone else?"***

CREATE HEROIC SERVICE GIVERS

I conclude where I began. Providing exemplary customer service requires heroism. It requires that the men and women you employ perform above and beyond the call of duty. You must be a hero. You must ensure that your staff are heroes. This takes training, trust, rewards and more training.

After driving our Hertz rented car for about 40 minutes, we realized our request for air conditioning had not been met. Rather than return to Heathrow Airport in London, England, where we had picked up the car, we pulled into the first branch office we saw. The manager, hearing our story, called the airport branch and was told no substitute could be found. She went on to call several other area branches. Once a suitable car was located, she asked us to follow her to the branch. She arranged everything inside, transferred our luggage and guided us back to the highway. She also put in a complaint on our behalf. Back in Canada, we received a letter of apology and a $50 voucher.

> *(Service is)...taking care of all the details. True service may be unseen and unheard—but it never goes unnoticed.*
>
> Sam Geist

View customer service as a circle. It has no beginning. It has no end.

- *It is an ongoing search for problematic areas, areas that require improvement, areas you anticipate will require improvement.*

- *It is getting feedback internally from your staff. **Do they agree?** It is getting feedback externally from your customers. **Are you all on the same wavelength?***

Note: *This is a relationship-building process. It strengthens bonds.*

- *It is using the information collected, using your own intuition, your years of experience to make changes, to get better.*

View customer service as an investment. A good investment. *It is.* In a recent *Harvard Business Review* article, researchers indicated that a 5 percent increase in customer retention *(acquired I'm certain because of customer service)* resulted in a 25-to-80 percent increase in profits. The value of exemplary customer service drops right to your bottomline.

View customer service as the ultimate profit center. It doesn't spoil, it has no expiry date, it occupies no shelf space. Service is the miracle solution for business success today—*and tomorrow.*

As a consultant and speaker to many business groups who are looking for ways to increase their overall profitability, I suggest they abandon the concept of service, the perspective of being a service provider, and adopt instead the banner of a "solution provider." It is indeed solutions that today's customers seek, solutions to their problems. Provide them and you'll find memorable service just automatically is the result.

Finally, view customer service as integral to your business, as Wolfgang Puck, well known chef & restaurateur, does.

"I always tell my cooks that one of the main ingredients in their food is the waiter, because it is the waiter who presents the food to the customer."

INSTITUTE A SERVICE ACTION-PLAN

Create a plan that works for you—your staff—your customers. The following suggestions may prove to be useful in implementing your plan—then *execute! Execute! Execute!*

1. **Use a "wish list" to stay close to customers.**

    Ask customers to list the five things that are most important to them. List their most frequent answers. Take the top 20 percent and ask customers to prioritize them. **Is your plan in sync with your customers' answers?** *Get it together!*

2. **Encourage customer complaints.**

    Track customer complaints. Use their feedback to improve your performance. *(Note: In Nordstrom, the department store chain, the service counter is on the first floor at the front, not hidden in a corner of an upper floor).* Don't defend. Correct problems. Statistics show that 50-to-70 percent of dissatisfied customers who have their complaints remedied, return, whereas less than 10 percent of those who do not air their complaints and subsequently they are not solved, ever return to do business again.

    Measure customer satisfaction. Very often customers don't bother to complain at all when they make small purchases. They just buy somewhere else next time.

> *When it comes to pleasing customers, it doesn't matter whether they're right or wrong. What matters is solving the problem at hand.*
>
> Jeffrey Mount, President
> Wright's Gourmet House
> *Inc.*

A 1987 study conducted by Leo Burnett, a British advertising agency revealed:

- *91 percent of customers who received really bad service wouldn't return*

- *86 percent of customers would go out of their way to shop where service is better*

- *70 percent of customers would even be willing to pay a little more for their purchases if service was particularly good.*

3. **Stay in touch after the sale.**

   Establish a vibrant relationship. Concentrate on tangibilizing the intangible.

4. **Go hi-tech.**

   Use new technology—record up-to-date details of your customers' needs and buying habits. You will be able to respond quickly.

   Banks across the United States are responding by installing next generation ATMs *(automated teller machines)* to enhance the value of the financial services they give their customers.

   Not only do the Super ATMs dispense cash, they make change, cash cheques to the penny and are equipped to dispense a variety of items from stamps to traveler cheques to movie tickets. The "customiz-able" software gives the banks the flexibility to install the features *their* customers would appreciate.

5. **Use mystery shoppers.**

    By shopping at your business, or utilizing your services, they'll provide you with an objective report of what they found in your organization. Get recommendations. Make calls. Do "walk throughs." Institute recommendations.

6. **Ask customers how you're doing every day**.

    Talk to them. Use questionnaires. Give out feedback forms. Ask customers to compare you with your competitors.

7. **Hold staff meetings frequently and regularly.**

    Share information. Make your staff knowledgeable. Make them experts.

8. **Find new creative ways to stay in touch.**

    Check out what your competitors are doing and improve on it. Check out what other industries do and adapt it. Find out what your staff and customers think and implement it.

9. **Meet your promises.**

    Make promises that are important to your customers. Make only promises you can keep—and then move heaven and earth to meet them.

    Kept promises build trust and cement bonds, just as overpromising and underdelivering destroys customer bonds and loyalty.

Promises include basics like company policies:

- *Return Policy (one that is fair and upfront and flexible, the kind of policy that encourages customers to return).*

- *Contact Policy, a promise that says if your 1-800 number is available 24 hours daily, it is.*

A good friend decided to make a Thanksgiving turkey dinner—with all the trimmings. He was stumped by the directions on the stuffing box and asked me to help him out. I phoned 1-800-TURKEY STUFFING, the number indicated on the stuffing package, in hope of getting assistance on Thanksgiving Day. Only an answering machine was available to take my inquiry. I also phoned 1-800-TURKEY the number on the turkey wrapper, and was again frustrated. It was only when I reached 1-800-OCEAN SPRAY *(the cranberry sauce company)* and the line was answered by a company representative did I realize that your *contact policy* promises are as important to the customer as your *in-store salesperson* promises.

Promises also include company credibility:

- *Promises of quality, of value, of product/service performance (your word is your guarantee).*

Not only do your promises count, promises made by your staff count too. Promises are not forgotten. Don't make any you can't keep, no matter how good your intentions. In a marketplace fraught with competition, a promise failed is a customer lost.

10. Pay attention to details.

It's all the small things that add up to outstanding customer service.

Details! Details! Details!

Sam Geist

- *It's using their name whenever you talk to customers.*

- *It's keeping in-touch after the sale is made to check on customers' satisfaction.*

- *It's giving customers something occasionally, rather than only selling them something.*

- *It's letting loyal customers know first about a sale, a particularly good deal, new merchandise or service.*

- *It's maintaining your image so it remains in sync with your customers; in this way maintaining the relationship makes them feel good about themselves.*

- *It's keeping the promises you make.*

- *It's remembering that any relationship is maintained only as long as it's of benefit to the people involved.*

- *It's things like cleanliness and neatness and honesty and trust.*

11. Lead. Teach by example.

The more you demonstrate your commitment to pleasing customers the higher is your staff's motivation to do the same.

Train staff to adopt a "customer-first" attitude. In every field where staff really served customers, they themselves benefited.

Teach staff by example, who the really big bosses are, and why it is necessary to provide them with the kind of service that makes them happy, encourages them to return, keeps them loyal.

12. Check your company's level of customer service.

Make anonymous telephone inquiries. If the responses are not satisfying *to you*, do something about it. *(Staff who answer your phone are a major competitive asset—or liability).*

13. Be in control operationally.

However, encourage flexibility in customer service so staff can utilize their own good sense and their experience. Support their service initiatives.

At all times, use your own best judgment.

Nordstrom employee handbook

14. Create incentives.

Encourage staff to behave in ways which serve customer interests. Eliminate incentives that do not.

15. There is no magic formula for customer service.

It takes time, effort, enormous commitment, know-how and follow-up. It takes thinking "solutions."

Customer service really is the final frontier in business today. Providing it effectively, beneficially, better than anyone else in that three feet of territory *(that small face-to-face space)* between you and your customer is the most straightforward route to customer satisfaction, to loyalty, to business longevity, to bottomline profitability. Talk is cheap. Action speaks louder than words.

Execution *is* the service strategy!

Answer that oft evaded question, **"Why should someone do business with you...rather than someone else?"**

> *If I go to a restaurant and the food is okay, but the service is great, then I'll go back. If the food is great but the people aren't, I won't go back —and I'm in the cooking profession.*
>
> Wolfgang Puck, chef and owner
> Spago restaurant
> *Successful Meetings*

ASK. ANSWER. PLAN. CHANGE.

From a customer service perspective, be sure to ask and answer these 21 questions.

1. **Why should someone do business with you...rather than someone else?**

_____

_____

_____

_____

2. **What is the definition of customer service in your organization? Who knows about this definition? Do customers agree it satisfies their needs?**

_____

_____

_____

_____

3. What particular service needs do your customers have?
    What particular service needs do you foresee your
    customers having next year or the year after that?
    What solutions are you providing for those needs?

_____

_____

_____

_____

_____

4. Who does a customer service "walk through" in your
    organization? How often? Who gets the feedback from
    the "walk through?" How is it used?

_____

_____

_____

_____

5. Where are the "moments of truth" in your
    organization? What are you doing to
    make them "moments of triumph?"

_____

_____

_____

_____

6. How effective is your organization/customer
    communication? When was the last time you checked
    if your customer service was in sync with your
    customers' expectations? What did you find out?

    _____

    _____

    _____

    _____

    _____

7. What are you doing to customer-ize your service?

    _____

    _____

    _____

8. What special benefits in your service strategy
    encourage customers to do business with you?

    _____

    _____

    _____

    _____

9. Do you know what your customers consider to be good
    value? What is their definition of good value?

    _____

    _____

    _____

    _____

10. What do you do to deliver good value? Is there anything else you can do?

_____

_____

_____

_____

11. What new opportunities can you create for your organization based on your customers' definition of good value?

_____

_____

_____

_____

12. Have you set clear customer service standards within your business? What are they? Who knows about these standards?

_____

_____

_____

_____

13. What steps can you take to eradicate the staff indifference that drives customers away?

_____

_____

_____

_____

14. How are customer complaints handled? Is the
    information recorded? Discussed? Where is your
    customer complaint department located?

    _____

    _____

    _____

    _____

    _____

15. What service techniques do you use, do your staff use,
    to stay in touch with your customers—after the sale—
    after the service is performed?

    What can you do to stay in touch that you are not
    currently doing?

    _____

    _____

    _____

    _____

    _____

16. What new technologies are you using to better enable
    you to serve your customers? What new technologies
    are you using to optimize the service they receive?

    _____

    _____

    _____

    _____

    _____

17. How do you rate the execution of your service strategy
    on a scale of one to ten? What can you do to make
    it a 10?

_____

_____

_____

_____

18. Do your customer service policies and standards
    accurately reflect who you are? Do they accurately
    reflect who you want to be?

_____

_____

_____

_____

19. What is your competitors' customer service like?
    Have you checked? How recently? What can you learn?

_____

_____

_____

20. Does your mission statement include a service
    component? Does everyone in your business know
    and understand your mission statement?

_____

_____

_____

_____

21. Do you give recognition to your customer service heroes? How? How often?

_____

_____

_____

_____

Write in one additional question you feel is important to you, your situation as a result of reading this section—*and then answer it.*

Q. _____

_____

_____

_____

_____

_____

_____

A. _____

_____

_____

_____

_____

_____

Part five is a practical, ready-to-apply section focusing on the issue of staff as ambassador or assassin. Some of the many techniques detailed to create a productive workplace include: effective motivators to encourage productivity — simple-to-use recognition suggestions — a training program checklist. Also investigated is the destructive influence of miscommunication. A discussion of the art of selling provides specific answers to *"Why should someone do business with you...rather than someone else?"*

Frontline = Bottomline 5

Are your staff ambassadors or assassins?

The last 30 years have taught me that we live or die through our frontline people. They decide why—*or why not*—someone should do business with you...rather than someone else.

They either propel you upward to new heights, or they drag you down. I see them quite clearly as ambassadors—or assassins. Ambassadors are your staff, your salespeople, your envoys—your representatives to the big boss, *your customers*. These diplomats help to build your image, your reputation, your organization and your bottomline.

Assassins, however, destroy whatever gets in the way—the relationship you have developed with your customers, the trust, the image, the reputation you have built up. Assassins drive customers away. They are dangerous to the good health of your organization.

> *Motivate employees, train them, care about them, and make winners of them. At Marriott, we know that if we treat our employees correctly, they'll treat the customers right. And if the customers are treated right, they'll come back.*
>
> Bill Marriott, Jr., Chairman
> Marriott Hotels

We can all vividly recall entering one of our favorite restaurants, only to endure shabby service, by a new waiter.

We can all vividly recall waiting all day for the repairperson who never called and never showed up.

We can all vividly recall being ignored by sales staff while they continue to chat on the phone.

They are your assassins! *You always remember assassins.*

A real-life story. To keep up, I often read out-of-town newspapers while flying. Unfortunately this preoccupation leaves me with ink-stained hands. On an American Airlines flight to Dallas, Texas, I asked a stewardess, who was making her way down the aisle, for a wet nap. I held up my hands, as an explanation. She said she was sorry there were no wetnaps and gave me a "what-can-I-do?" look. I suggested a wet napkin might do. She promptly grabbed some from her cart, thoroughly dousing them with water. Gingerly she handed the wad, dripping wet, over Doug Olsen, from GE Capital, who was sitting in the aisle seat next to me—splashing him in the process. I happily cleaned my hands and then requested another napkin to dry them. By this time the cart was gone. No napkins. She looked uncertain of how to handle this new challenge. With a sudden smile, she reached over and turned on my overhead air vent full blast. "Hold them under there," she said. Doug was quick to retort, "Give him some shampoo and he can wash his hair too." Her ineptitude made her American Airlines' assassin.

We can all vividly recall the customer service consultant who said they would straighten out the mess on our phone bill...*and did.*

We all vividly recall the salesperson who called every one of the company's locations to find the coat we wanted in our size.

We all vividly recall the doctor's receptionist who made arranging the tests we needed, their top priority, because they saw how worried we were.

They are your ambassadors! *You always remember ambassadors.*

Another real-life story. While conducting a seminar in Appleton, Wisconsin, I stayed at the Paper Valley Hotel & Conference Center. Program concluded, I checked out, jumped into a cab and headed for the airport. Shortly after I arrived, I heard over the intercom that a message was waiting for me. The hotel's manager had driven out to deliver a fax that had arrived after my departure. He wanted to ensure I didn't miss any important information. He was the hotel's ambassador.

Interestingly, whether your staff are your assassins or your ambassadors depends to a great extent on you.

Whether you endure high staff turnover or not depends to a great extent on you.

I recently consulted for a company whose rate of turnover, below managerial level, was 145 percent in one year. Imagine

The hardest customer to turn on is your employee.

Sam Geist

the chaos, the wasted investment, the low morale, the dismal service.

Finding, hiring, holding onto ambassadors takes know-how, skill and planning, no matter whether your organization is small or large. The commitment to find, hire and hold onto ambassadors spreads through the ranks quickly.

It all starts by getting to know your staff—*well.* Get to know:

- *Who they really are.*

- *Where they come from.*

- *What they want and need.*

- *What concerns them (aside from making a good living).*

- *What their demographic and psychographic characteristics are.*

- *How these characteristics and everything else you've learned about them, affect their performance.*

Get to know them as well as you know your customers.

WANTS AND NEEDS

At the top of most employee "wants and needs" list is job security. Wherever we look, employees are either checking to ensure their job has not disappeared or are too busy to check because they've been asked to take on the roles of departed cohorts as well. Required to do more with less, they are apprehensive about succeeding. Today's employees are stretched, stressed and insecure.

They are looking for job protection. Cliff Hakim, author of *We Are All Self-Employed* makes these suggestions to staff:

Network.

Stay in touch with colleagues and potential employers. It encourages opportunities to be discovered.

Coach.

Use a career counselor to assess strengths and to identify weaknesses, enabling positive change to be achieved.

Save.

Have a financial cushion, to allow for desirable choices and options to be exercised.

Everyone wants a good salary, but the wants and needs highlighted most frequently by the employees questioned, are job fulfillment, recognition by superiors and co-workers and a feeling of empowerment— all on-the-job conditions.

There's a special purgatory for service businesses that forget their business starts with people. What happened [to Wendy's] was typical. Managers weren't getting the respect they needed and were passing their frustrations along to the crew. The crew felt unappreciated, made the customers feel the same, and they voted with their feet.... It was time to heave charts and concentrate on the basics. Beginning with the most basic of all: Mop Bucket Attitude, or M.B.A. Mop Bucket Attitude says... quarterly earnings have no meaning to the customer, but quality food, variety, and atmosphere do.

James Near, former Chairman and CEO
Wendy's International

When Michael Smith became CEO at Lands' End, times were tough for the catalog company. Instead of using a slash 'n' burn technique, he has done the opposite. He has invested to improve quality and increase employee benefits. Smith feels it makes sense because their customers will pay for great quality sold by employees who pamper them. "If people feel squeezed, they won't treat the customer as well."

When 3,000 employers were asked in a study conducted by the National Center on the Educational Quality of the Workforce what was at the top of their "employee should have" list, they included:

■ *good attitude and ability to communicate effectively*

■ *previous work experience*

■ *recommendation from current employer*

When employees learn what their employers want and need, when employers understand what their employees want and need, and when they both understand what customers want and need—they can work together to satisfy those customers—*their ultimate boss—better.*

To determine level of service demonstrated and to discover what barriers there were to providing memorable service, I conducted research with manufacturers and service

---

BARRIERS TO GOOD PERFORMANCE
1. Don't know what is expected of them.
2. Don't know how to do something.
3. Don't want to do something.
4. Don't have the proper tools, equipment or instructions for the job.
5. Don't know that they aren't performing well.
6. Don't have the ability or are overqualified for it.

Sam Geist

organizations where the majority of staff work in isolation from their final customers. From my experience I found staff in isolated environments often fail to satisfy their customers because they lack the opportunity to find out if their customers are happy or not *and why*. Frequently, they don't realize what it is that satisfies, that satisfying is part of their job, or indeed, that they themselves didn't satisfy.

Your responsibility is to identify the ability of potential staff, to mobilize their energy and assist them to focus this energy toward your high standards.

Your staff, like everyone else on the planet, need to be motivated—recognized for their skills, their contribution and rewarded for their efforts, their successes. Encourage your staff to take on the role of ambassadors by motivating them.

> *You can take my factories, burn up my building, but give me my people and I'll build the business right back again.*
>
> Henry Ford, (1863-1947), founder Ford Motor Company, Inc.

Bob Nelson, V.P. of Blanchard Training & Development Inc. feels that staff are motivated by "intangible variables like full appreciation for a job well done, being part of decisions that affect them, open communication, interesting and meaningful work and having good relationships at work."

On my top 10 list for effective motivators are suggestions to provide intangible variables as well as some tangible ones.

> *It's a company's responsibility to allow each individual to be as good as he or she is capable of being. People basically want to do a good job. I have never heard anybody walk out of this building and say, "Boy, I feel great! I did a lousy job today."*
>
> Harvey Miller, Co-owner
> Quill Corporation
> *Nation's Business*

> *Rotating people and letting them work in different assignments is an excellent way to keep a person's work interesting. In addition, it serves to enrich and develop the employee's skills. It's a pity that it isn't practiced more broadly.*
>
> Andrew S. Grove, CEO
> Intel Corporation
> *One-On-One with Andy Grove*

TOP 10 MOTIVATORS FOR A PRODUCTIVE WORKPLACE

1. **Recognize, reward** and promote high performers; **motivate** low or marginal performers to improve *(or ask to leave if improvement does not happen)*. Use a team approach. It inspires productivity.

2. **Break large, demanding projects into smaller manageable chunks.** This technique ensures there is always light at the end of the tunnel. Assessment at the conclusion of a smaller segment, rather than the whole, gives those involved the opportunity to check their performance and make any necessary adjustments in order to stay on track. Acknowledge completion of each segment. Recognizing effort, boosts morale and reinforces commitment and interest.

3. **Train.** Encourage staff to acquire new skills, new abilities. Demonstrate how both the organization's and individual's goals can be achieved.

   Cross-train. In today's "light" organizations, where the number of staff has been greatly reduced, the need for change is translated as the need to be competent in several areas, rather than just one. Staff must be able to broaden their area of expertise.

4. **"Technolog-ize" the organization.** Make it efficient. Create a state-of-the-art operation with trained, skilled, up-to-date staff who provide a competitive advantage.

5. **Empower staff** to make decisions, especially in the specific areas that affect them. Commitment follows closely on the heels of involvement. Convey a sense of ownership to staff in their work and their work environment, even if this ownership is only symbolic, by creating a "career" mentality, rather than a "putting-in-time" attitude. Salary may not keep pace with ownership status, but pride and commitment and performance will.

6. **Be up front** about the organization's operation, products, services, future goals, strategies for achieving them and profit-and-loss picture. Outline staff's role in the plan.

To perform effectively, groups also need at least a minimal belief in their own efficacy.... Believing both that a job is important and that it can be done easily lead group members to behave more aggressively.

Gregory P. Shea, The Wharton School & Richard Guzzo, New York University
Sloan Management Review

Align Troops Behind the Vision
- *turn employees to teammates/crew members*
- *turn part timers into support staff*
- *turn job descriptions into job responsibilities*
- *turn work into career path*
- *turn putting in time into ownership*

Sam Geist

> **Good words are worth much, and cost little.**
>
> George Herbert, (1593-1632),
> English clergyman & poet
> *Jacula Prudentum*

7. **Thank staff** for a job well done. A thank you goes a long way—thank in person, in writing or publicly in your organization's newsletter. Do it often. Do it as soon after the job has been done as possible.

8. **Create a pleasant work environment** that is open, fun. Assist staff to take the initiative. Lend an empathetic ear. Listen to employees suggestions, ideas, problems, grievances. Then take action.

9. **Assess. Revise.** Establish realistic expected productivity levels. Maximize but don't crush. Ask staff for group input. Consider their suggestions.

10. **Celebrate successes,** whether they be organizational, departmental or personal. Reward them.

Look inside your organization. **What motivators do you provide?**

Add these motivators to your checklist and begin to make the changes needed so you can rate yourself excellent, and so your employees will rate you as excellent.

Create a strong, empathetic bond. John Naisbitt, author of *Megatrends*, writing on the alienating impact today's technology has on the workplace, comments "the more high-tech around us, the more the need for human touch."

The human touch recognizes staff as individuals, as people.

Without this recognition staff may leave, or stay and work with reduced commitment.

I often speak to organizations that are trying to motivate staff but feel they are not successful at achieving their objectives. After some probing, it often appears that the key missing element is recognition and reward.

Here's how some organizations motivate through recognition and reward. Adapt their ideas to your own situation.

Haworth Inc., an office furniture manufacturer, in Holland, Michigan, decided to implement a formal suggestion program after it read the statistics of the Employee Involvement Association, revealing that organizations using these programs show savings of $33,500 per 100 employees. Employees at Haworth were permitted to implement their ideas after informing their supervisors or were encouraged to work with staff in other departments to implement ideas directly concerning their jobs. Since the inauguration of the program in 1991, results at Haworth show that suggestions per employee jumped to 2.39 from .79 suggestions and in 1994 savings, based on

Formal performance appraisal plans are designed to meet three needs, one for the organization and two for the individual:
1. They provide systematic judgments to back up salary increases, promotions, transfers and sometimes demotions or terminations.
2. They are a means of telling a subordinate how he is doing, and suggesting needed changes in his behavior, attitudes, skills, or job knowledge; they also let him know "where he stands" with the boss.
3. They are being increasingly used as a basis for the coaching and counseling of the individual by the superior.

Douglas McGregor, (1879-1964), Professor of Management, M.I.T. and President of Antioch College
Harvard Business Review

employee suggestions, were in the $8 million range.

Recognition and reward for implemented suggestions are often financial. Some organizations give cash incentives, while others offer share of profits for ideas that go to market.

Recognition and reward validate for staff that their knowledge and opinions are worthwhile. This not only assists productivity, but also boosts staff morale.

Tom Terry, a Bell Atlantic employee whose suggestion was the largest revenue producer to come from the employee suggestion program, remarked "Being able to see something I've done become visible in the company was the primary motivator."

We give a bonus for the employees to give them a sense of participation and to feel that they are members of the company because we are always saying our company has one fate. If the company goes well, everybody can enjoy. If the company goes wrong or bankrupt, people lose jobs.

Akio Morita, CEO
Sony Corporation (Japan)
Cherry Blossoms and Robotics

John Longstreet, of the Harvey Hotel in Plano, Texas took a slightly different approach to motivate through recognition. He established "what's stupid?" meetings, randomly choosing six to eight employees to discuss "what's stupid?" with the way the hotel was being run. His objective was "to encourage employees to understand that there are things we could do better and they are the best ones to tell me about them."

Surprising perhaps, but certainly beneficial to the hotel, is the fact that most of the ideas that Longstreet culls are ways to improve customer service rather than ways for staff to improve their own situation.

Staff are also motivated and become "loyalized" when they are recognized just for being themselves, just for being part of your workforce.

Adapt and use these ideas to acknowledge and inspire your staff. Create and implement your own ideas.

In our culture, these [service] jobs are not considered a worthwhile occupation. When workers view giving service as beneath them, it shows.

Thomas Kelly, Assistant Professor
Cornell University, School of
Hotel Administration

TEN REALLY SIMPLE RECOGNITION IDEAS

1. Send birthday cards to staff *(signed by the boss, of course)* *Note:* as a corollary, send a small gift, flowers, candy, cake, cookies, etc.

2. Give staff a birthday "sleep in" *(come to work later)* or leave earlier in the day *(out by 3 pm)*. Offer them a "dress down" day.

3. Acknowledge staff's anniversary date with the company with a card, a bottle of wine or other treat. It's an important date to them.

4. Recognize longtime staff with a celebration. Present and hang a framed photograph of the recipient on an honor wall. A group dinner can be part of the festivities.

5. Hold an awards ceremony on a regular basis and present certificates, badges, pins or plaques for "the-best-of" and for

"excellence" to deserving staff. Invite family and friends to attend.

6. Reward outstanding performance *(as noted by a customer)* with theater/movie passes, dinner vouchers, etc.

7. Feature "the best of" or "excellent performance" in your organization's newsletter.

8. Print business cards for staff as a method of recognizing their role in the organization.

9. Publicize special achievements through public relations releases to local media *(radio, TV, newspapers)*.

10. Bring in lunch, bagels or donuts just because you appreciate your staff.

Some ideas of your own:

_____

_____

_____

_____

_____

_____

_____

_____

_____

_____

_____

_____

Recognizing your staff, costs very little, but it can do much to build morale, instill passion, boost energy, develop the attitude that encourages someone to do business with you, and ultimately contribute to the bottomline.

TO TRAIN...OR NOT TO TRAIN

You are only as good as the people you train.

Lonear Heard, President
James T. Heard Management Corporation
Black Enterprise

To train or not to train staff isn't the real question. The real question is To Be in business in the year 2000 or Not To Be in business. If you are interested in remaining in business for the long term, then by all means train. *It's that simple.*

Smart organizations realize that to keep up with their competitors and to successfully meet tomorrow's challenges, their leaders must be well informed. They must change, learn, know.

Organizations also realize that their staff must be as knowledgeable and as well informed in *their areas of expertise* as the top brass is in theirs. Their staff's knowledge and professionalism are their biggest assets. Smart organizations realize the transitory nature of skills and training today. On-going education and on-the-job training are a fact of corporate life that must be conducted with commitment and dedication for the long-term well being of both the organization and its staff.

Your customers see you through your staff. Your staff represent your attitude, your image, so hire staff who see eye to eye

> *To improve a company fast, develop people fast.*
>
> Andrew E. Pearson, Past President
> PepsiCo
> *The Renewal Factor*

with you on the fundamentals of your business and then be prepared to train from hiring day onward. Train for building and growth.

McDonald's, at its Hamburger U, provides courses in topics such as team building, staffing and retention. The courses have been compared to an MBA crash course. McDonald's takes its service seriously.

McDonald's Chicago meat supplier, OSI Industries, operates under joint ventures in 17 countries including Bavaria. The need to train staff, to ensure consistently excellent quality, is as necessary in Bavaria as it is in Chicago. OSI International President, Douglas Gullang, says, "Meeting McDonald's standards is a huge challenge. To some, it seems insane what we do. But we realize our product isn't just meat, it's service. We've turned a meat plant into a service business."

Empower staff with real training so they have the skills, the knowledge, the techniques to do their job well. It is only through training that staff learn the fundamentals of your business, such as: what the equipment specifications are, who would help out in an emergency, what the warranty on the equipment is and how the service contract works *(in other words—the promises you made—the promises that must be kept)*.

It is only through training, that staff realize and practice the social and psychological nuances that separate the ambassadors from the assassins. It is only through training that they acquire communication skills to know how, *and why*, to treat a young Boomer differently from a Senior. It is only through training that they learn how to mollify and satisfy an angry customer rather than inflame them.

In a 1996 *USA Today* interview, respondents were asked what they thought would protect them in an unstable environment. Most frequently, they replied it was to participate in on-the-job training. Staff welcome training, because it increases their value in the job market. A large percentage feel it is an excellent form of compensation, in many cases more valuable than financial reward.

Large training companies recommend that 5 percent of each employees' work week should be devoted to training, to upgrading. Give and you shall receive. Expect and you shall get.

Studies show that the fastest growing U.S. organizations commonly spend about five times the national average on training. They know investing in staff training pays big dividends later. They realize that by doing their staff good, they are also doing themselves good. Well trained staff give the competitive edge needed to succeed in today's fast changing markets. Training, including the opportunity to learn about new technology, encourages staff to stay, because their work environment is satisfying.

With rampant job insecurity, upgrading skills and on-going

Hire for attitude.
Train for skill.

training alleviate fear of job attrition. Staff with up-to-the minute training and skills feel they would be able to relocate, if necessary, without traumatic hardship—eliminating their stress and allowing staff to concentrate on work at hand.

John Krol, President of DuPont recognizes, "One of our responsibilities is to make sure employees are given the skills and experience to 'progress' either inside the company or outside the company."

Because the needs, expectations, demands and specifics in every organization are different, new staff must be trained. A cursory "show-around" is not good enough. Give new staff the skills to do the job for which they were hired. After all, you spent the money advertising the position, the time interviewing, and you're going to be paying them for a long time. New staff need to know what your organization is all about. They need to appreciate your corporate culture and understand their role within this environment. Give experienced staff the up-to-date information and skills development they need to continue doing their best.

Your holiness, how many
people work in the Vatican?
About half!
Pope John XXIII

Some organizations fake training by sending around memoranda about skills improvement once in a while, or by holding "quicky" discussions at lunch or after work – on a less than occasional basis. Both the organization and the staff pay the price, because at the end of the day, everyone is left holding a tinsel wrapped Easter egg. Bright glitzy wrapper *(the promise of things to come)*, thin layer of chocolate *(the teaser)*, and of course the hollow interior.

Some organizations feel training is not an essential investment. They are hesitant to train either because it's costly for trainers, in time and materials, or because they fear that expertised staff may not stay. They are afraid the benefit of their training may go to their competitor. They ask why not just recruit skilled employees away from their competitors? Called the "free rider" problem by economists, this attitude may ultimately result in training not being given at all, leaving crucial skills in short supply and the organization or the industry seriously disadvantaged.

> ***Give people the ability to do what they would want to do if they only knew they could do it.***
>
> Daniel Burrus, author
> *Technotrends*
> Power Selling Conference and Symposium

In the long run, isn't lack of teaching, lack of training a tremendous risk? The price of staff telling customers "I don't know...it's not my department," the cost of being unable to quickly and correctly answer customers' questions, the results of making poor decisions based on faulty or incomplete knowledge, *is enormous!*

I'm allergic to shellfish. I never eat shrimp, lobster, crab or any crustaceans that inhabit the seas. While visiting my daughter in

> ***The expense isn't what it costs to train employees. It's what it costs not to train them.***
>
> Philip Wilber, President
> Drug Emporium, Inc.
> *Inc.*

Chicago, we decided to eat at The Big Bowl, an Asian restaurant specializing in Japanese and Thai noodle soups. My daughter, a vegetarian, asked our waitress why their vegetable noodle pot was not asterisked as vegetarian? The waitress replied, that the stock was made of fish. We queried her, fish stock or shellfish stock? Is someone allergic to shellfish, she queried back quickly? When I explained my allergy, she pointed out on my menu exactly what I could eat— two dishes. She explained that she was trained so she knew what ingredients were in each dish. I was grateful. I imagined the consequences of untrained, uninformed wait staff and shuddered.

I recently spoke at a Photo Marketing Association Conference and to prepare for the presentation I conducted retail research. Disguised as a customer in search of the new widely touted APS *(Advanced Photo System)* camera, I visited half a dozen camera shops. I asked questions—after all I wanted to make a big purchase. I asked *why should I buy this type of camera? What were its advantages? How was it different from conventional photographic apparatus?* Not one salesperson made me feel comfortable enough to buy.

Hundreds of millions of dollars were spent on development. Millions are being spent on advertising. Thousands are being spent on store rent and fixtures and inventory. Very little, however, seems to be spent on training, so that the link between development and purchase can be satisfactorily completed.

As consumers, we need to have confidence in the knowledge, in the expertise of those with whom we interact. We need to know that pilots and doctors and line workers and waiters and frontline people have the information, the knowledge to serve us well.

> *Doing depends upon learning, not learning upon doing. [Therefore] learning must precede practice.*
>
> Jerusalem Talmud, Peschim

Manpower, the temp agency, has been proving the value of training because it regards training as a two-way street. By teaching workers the skills they need, it finds the workers return for more training.

DeVry and other technical training institutes have also grown by filling the technology gap. They supply a technically skilled workforce to smaller technology-based companies, traditionally burdened with undertrained staff that prevented them from capitalizing on emerging opportunities.

Training, in addition to providing much-needed, much-demanded skills, provides other desirable benefits.

It creates for the organization the opportunity to effectively communicate and re-assert its corporate vision through its staff.

It opens the organization to improvement, since training provides new alternatives to the old ways of operating. Training facilitates everything from creating new ways to serve customers better—to developing new marketing strategies—to streamlining internal organizational systems. It clarifies staff roles. For example, grocery stock clerks often regard their role as

> *Some people are excited about learning a new piece of software. Other people get very depressed. Good managers anticipate both situations— they involve the persons to be affected in the process of selecting a particular program, and they provide time and resources for training. Training is the key in both cases.*
>
> Jonathan P. Siegel,
> Information Communications Associates
> *Communications*

a purely utilitarian one—keeping the shelves stocked. With this perspective of their function, they come to regard and treat customers asking for information as an annoyance, an obstruction to getting their job— shelf-stocking— accomplished. Effective training outlines the broader spectrum of their responsibility.

Train with specific goals in mind. Outline these goals clearly.

Inform. Teach technical skills, including "how-to" *and* "why-to". Share your corporate vision.

Like the tenets governing superior leadership, efficient operations, value-added products and services, effective training must be constantly revised and updated to remain on the cutting edge.

Structure training programs according to time and needs constraints, but insist that two criteria be met—always. *First,* develop a specific, focused schedule. *Second,* require mandatory attendance. In order to succeed, the importance of the programs must be firmly established up-front and maintained throughout.

A TRAINING PROGRAM CHECKLIST

Before beginning, examine the program and its goals. Focus on these 10 vital considerations:

1. Does the program teach staff what their general and specific roles are, how their roles relate to other staff and how they relate to the organization as a whole?

2. Does the program specify the significance of their role *(keeping in mind that everyone, everywhere wants to feel important)?*

3. Does the program clearly outline the organization's vision and corporate culture? Does it explain the role of training in maintaining it?

4. Does the program teach staff the necessity of increasing customer retention for the organization? Their role in achieving this vital goal?

5. Does the program explain the expectations and demands of the organization's customers? Does it teach staff how to focus on these expectations and demands?

6. Does the program explain why customers buy? Does it teach staff how their attitudes, behavior, actions affect the buying decision and their customers' perception of quality?

7. Does the program teach customer-focused attitudes in order to deliver consistent and reliable service? Does it

include a segment for frontline staff that stresses the importance of incorporating customer-focused selling techniques in order to improve selling effectiveness and relationship building?

8. **Does the program stress the importance of developing inter-personal skills to facilitate a team approach?**

9. **Does the program teach how to effectively handle confrontational customers or how to overcome customers' objections or how to develop a long term customer-organization relationship?**

10. **Does the program detail the components for instituting, maintaining and soliciting customer feedback?**

A *"yes"* to all 10 questions ensures an excellent training program has been developed.

Implement training on an on-going basis, assessing, evaluating and updating it regularly, adjusting objectives and goals as needs change. A carefully crafted, finely executed program is a most effective way to lead the pack. It is a sure way to make dust—rather than eat it.

No matter the logistics of the program, or who its trainers are, the ultimate goal for effective training, for beneficial learning, is to get everyone in the organization singing, not lip-syncing, clearly, in tune with smiling assurance, from the same song sheet.

> *You can change behavior in an entire organization, provided you treat training as a process rather than an event.*
>
> Edward W. Jones, training director
> General Cinema Beverage
> *Training*

Training is not a "cure all." When malaise strikes an organization, however, providing training "to fix" the situation is traditionally the route undertaken. The answer usually *is* training, but two other possibilities exist as cause for the difficulties—*lack of resources* and *lack of motivation*. When internal staff problems arise, making an assessment before making a diagnosis and offering a solution, speeds up recovery.

Ask yourself these questions to determine where the problem lies and hence where the solution may be found.

> *Training won't cover up for poor equipment and outmoded methods. It won't offset mediocre products or deteriorating markets. It won't compensate for poor compensation or abusive supervisory or management practices. And training definitely won't turn the unwilling and uncaring in your organization into motivated, devoted, gung-ho fireballs.*
>
> Ron Zemke, President
> Performance Research Associates
> *Training*

1. **Does your problem staff member understand their role in the organization?**

   (a "no" answer indicates a need for training)

2. **Does your problem staff member know specifically what their job responsibility is?**

   (a "no" answer indicates a need for training)

3. **Does your problem staff member have the skills to perform the job?**

   (a "no" answer indicates a need for training)

4. **Does your problem staff member have available the needed resources and support to do the job?**

   (a "no" answer indicates a need for resources rather than training)

5. **Although your problem staff member is not satisfactorily doing the job, could they if it were a matter of life and death?**

   (a 'yes' answer indicates a need for motivation)

EMPOWER STAFF

Bosses have to believe that people are not to be managed. Projects are.

Gerri Cronin, consultant
Dale Carnegie Systems
Business Access

Empowerment affects the culture of an organization so dramatically that it deserves special attention.

Authors Warren Bennis and Michael Mische define empowerment in *The 21st Century Organization* as :

"...removing bureaucratic boundaries that box people in and keep them from making the most effective use of all their skills, experiences, energies and ambitions. It means allowing them to develop a sense of ownership over parts of the process that are uniquely their responsibility, while at the same time demanding that they accept a share of the broader responsibility and ownership of the whole process."

Many organizations agree with Bennis and Mische's definition. However creating an empowered environment requires much more than just agreement.

It requires:

> *When utility company employees can operate billion dollar nuclear reactors, but must have "management approval" to register themselves for a training class, empowerment hasn't gone very far.*
>
> A. Glenn Kiser, organizational consultant
> *Training*

- *Staff who are encouraged to participate, to voice their opinions freely, to suggest change. They have a specific, defined role to play.*

- *Staff who accept responsibilities for the decision-making process and the outcome of their decisions.*

- *Staff who are effectively trained, have the skills and the knowledge to do – to act.*

  Management must be committed to encourage staff to think on the job, to solve problems, to improve organizational processes, to boost profits. Only those with know-how can be empowered *to act.*

- *Staff who have been given parameters, effective guidelines within which to work, within which to make their decisions.*

- *Management who understand that empowerment is not a fait accompli. It must be regarded from a developmental perspective, as a living, changing process to be reviewed, assessed and improved again and again and again.*

> *Once an employee is empowered, management can never remove that power and return to close supervision, without losing the employee, or at least their good will and commitment.*
>
> Fraser McAllan, consultant/trainer
> Masterpiece Corporation

- *Management who understand that empowerment sets a precedent, since it directs the continued, participative decision-making process throughout the organization.*

Empowerment has reached such heights in some organizations that employees have been able to make fundamental operational changes. Chairman of GE, Jack Welch describes this development, as "boundary busting"—a graphically memorable description.

Empowerment is also credited with facilitating flexi-management to take hold. When staff are responsible for their own productivity, are willing and able to make on-the-job decisions, work with little supervision, and few rules, job configurations such as part-time, flexible hours, job sharing, working at home, even bringing kids to work, become possible.

Nabisco, realizing the competitive nature of attracting and keeping top talent, has made flexible work conditions a recruitment and retention issue by formalizing a Work/Life Initiative that provides flexible options.

At Fel-Pro, an auto gasket company in Illinois, employees who enjoyed similar flexible programs had the highest job performance evaluations and the lowest intentions of leaving the company, concluded University of Chicago researchers.

In this work environment, staff feel they are the organization's strongest asset and take their responsibilities and commitment to the organization very seriously. A five year national study of the changing workforce by Families and Work Institute in New York concurs:

> *"Workers are more loyal, more committed, more innovative and more satisfied with their jobs when they have more of a say in how to do their jobs and have more control over the scheduling of their work hours."*

Anne Panker, a work/family balance consultant agrees. She believes that flexible options pay out at the bottomline, because people feel in control, respected and empowered. Their work reflects this attitude.

If painting empowerment across your organization with a broad brush is too overwhelming a task, decide where you can begin using a finer stroke. **Where can you implement this marketplace development to your advantage, to the advantage of your staff, to the advantage of your customers?**

> *You blew it. For 25 years, all you got is my hands, for the same salary you could have had my brains.*
> (comments of a custodian on his retirement)
>
> Don Bagin, publisher,
> Frank Grazian, executive director
> Communication Briefings
> *Let's Employ Their Brains Too*

GIVE BENEFITS

After discussing, how to motivate, reward, recognize, train and empower staff during my seminar programs, invariably someone in the audience asks if there are any other methods to help keep good staff. There are—*think benefits.*

Today employees want—actually expect—benefits. Some benefits have already been mentioned. Others include plans that may carry health and life insurance components, stock options, outside training and education and profitability bonuses.

Benefits provide a valuable incentive to attract the best new staff, and assist in keeping those already employed. Staff morale, dedication and concern for the well being of the organization is improved, since staff feel management is interested and concerned about them, their welfare and their needs.

In fact, studies have indicated that employee-benefit plans are instrumental in reducing absenteeism, as well as minimizing staff turnover. Several large American organizations have taken the value to be derived from benefits, into the partnership arena, in order to firmly cement loyalty and encourage entrepreneurship in their staff.

For example, the growth of the Outback Steakhouse (*an Australian-themed steakhouse chain in the United States),* has been rapid and secure, thanks in large measure to its staff recruitment policies.

Bob Basham, President, explained, "We wanted good managers in there who would think like owners, so we made sure they had a big chunk of the action." It works. Managers have that entrepreneurial flame, acting as operating partners because they share in the bottomline. They stay, minimizing the operational turbulence that occurs when staff, especially management, is transient.

The Outback Steakhouse also experiences an exceptionally low kitchen and wait staff turnover—5.4 percent, in comparison to the national average of 30 to 40 percent. The advantages multiply exponentially. Staff who have been there longer, know their jobs better, work better as a team and are therefore able to serve customers better. As the wheel comes full circle, it stands to reason that customers who are served better, are more satisfied and return frequently. This, in fact, has been the case in this very popular restaurant chain.

Consider your staff with the same regard and concern that you do your customers. To keep them loyal, to keep them satisfied, to keep them doing their best, treat them like your most important ambassadors—because they are!

> *Surround yourself with very good people; listen; and never forget business is a commitment and a work of art.*
>
> Jeannine Guillevin-Wood, Chairman
> Guillevin International Inc.
> *Profit*

MISCOMMUNICATION DEBILITATES

More than 50 years ago, Winston Churchill said, *"The difference between mere management and leadership is communication."* Leaders must have integrity, values, creativity, a vision and an action plan. However, without the ability to communicate their character, their talent, their dreams and their plans, they and even more so, their organization, are doomed.

Regard communication with staff from complementary perspectives. **What can you learn from your staff and what do they need to learn from you? What is important to them? What do they need to know to do their job better? To get more satisfaction from doing it?** Communicate to staff, not only what is important to you *but why*, not only what you expect from them, *but why*.

Management has in its repetoire of resources many options to ensure ambassadorship. One avenue toward this goal however, is frequently neglected: *communicating clearly, effectively, accurately, beneficially with staff.*

Very often—too often—I am asked to consult in organizations where on the one hand management seems to be oblivious to the needs and goals of their staff, and on the other, staff doesn't understand what management's goals are or why they exist. Thick, high walls stand between them, eliminating the possibility of each hearing or understanding the other, preventing a united "win/win" approach from being taken.

In whatever we do, excellent communication skills are a powerful advantage. Because these skills are vital to personal and business success, indoctrination begins early in life and continues into staff training sessions that are conducted after years of employment.

Why is it then that we still fail to communicate beneficially? Why is it we all assume we're communicating in a "crystal clear" manner? Why is it we're absolutely amazed to find we've been totally misunderstood—that before our very eyes, huge brick walls of miscommunication have been erected?

One of the primary reasons for this disturbing state of affairs is that we don't really listen to what's being communicated to us. Most of the time we're busy thinking up earthshaking responses, advice, suggestions. In the meantime, the words—the ideas—the intentions of those with whom we're talking, disappear—dissipate into thin air.

A short but stinging tongue twister tells the tale.

Everybody, Somebody, Anybody, Nobody

There was an important job to be done

and Everybody was asked to do it.

Everybody was sure Somebody would do it.

Anybody could have done it but Nobody did it.

Somebody got angry about that because it was Everybody's job.

Everybody thought Anybody could do it,

but Nobody realized that Everybody wouldn't do it.

It ended up that Everybody blamed Somebody

When actually Nobody asked Anybody.

Miscommunication can be prevented, or once entrenched, it can be obliterated by using a "Pay-Attention" strategy which includes both verbal and non-verbal components.

The strategy states that:

- Careful listening to the words spoken is important, but of much greater importance is attention to tone of voice and body language.

- To further enhance accurate communication, it is helpful to know a little about the speaker's background *(their perspective, their interest in the situation, where they're coming from)*.

- "Reconfirmation" prevents "brick-wall-building." This involves paraphrasing the essential gist of what has been conveyed to ensure accurate interpretation before a response is given.

- "Double visioning" prevents "brick-wall-building." That is, look at the statement from *your* point of view and from the *speaker's* point of view. This enables you to question your own interpretation, and ask the speaker if your interpretation is indeed accurate, before you respond.

- "Playing dumb" is another technique to prevent "brick-wall-building." Ask the speaker to rephrase their statement or clarify it for you. It sounds like, "I'm not sure what you're asking, could you explain it to me again

> ***Communication is determined by:***
> - ***Words used—seven percent***
> - ***Intonation, pace, pitch, volume, etc. (the way the words are said)—38 percent***
> - ***Non-verbals: stance, facial expression, gestures, eye-contact—55 percent***
>
> *Boardroom Reports*

> ***How well we communicate is determined not by how well we say things but by how well we are understood.***
>
> Andrew S. Grove, CEO
> Intel Corporation
> *One-On-One with Andy Grove*

please." This technique is excellent because in addition to giving you additional insight into the situation, it gives you a breathing space to collect your thoughts before you respond.

By keeping communication lines clear of debris, debilitating misunderstanding is minimized. Management and staff alike can concentrate on the real task at hand, *working together to build the organization and assure their own future in it.*

The advent of the virtual organization and the resulting proliferation of communication via e-mail presents new challenges. Without the customary non-verbal cues, such as tone of voice and body language, non-verbal messages can easily be misinterpreted. Clear, specific, factually-oriented messages are essential, as is re-confirmation by the receiver.

> *The most important element in establishing a happy, prosperous atmosphere was an insistence upon open, free, and honest communications up and down the ranks of our management structure.*
>
> Harold Geneen, former CEO and author
> ITT
> *Managing*

TEN WAYS TO MAKE THE WALLS COME TUMBLING DOWN

1. Believe that a win/win solution is possible.

2. Be observant.

3. Act rather than talk. Actions break down walls faster than rhetoric.

4. Be aware that first impressions are remembered.

5. Practice two-way communication rather than monologuing.

6. Understand that information re-transmitted and re-re-transmitted loses much of its accuracy and reliability.

7. Be conscious of preconceived notions. Unlearn them.

8. Evaluate after communication is completed, not before.

9. Instruct clearly. Direct simply. Explain completely.

10. Listen actively. Reconfirm information.

Eradicate miscommunication for the benefit of the organization and everyone in it. This short tale, from Joe Griffith's, *Speaker's Library of Business Stories, Anecdotes and Humor*, hilariously reinforces the importance of accurate communication.

> *A young FBI man was put in charge of the FBI's supply department. In an effort to cut cost, he reduced the size of memo paper.*
>
> *One of the new memo sheets ended up on J. Edgar Hoover's desk. He disliked it immediately and wrote on the narrow margin, "Watch the borders."*
>
> *His message was misinterpreted. For the next six weeks, it was extremely difficult to enter the United States by road from either Mexico or Canada.*

THE ART OF SELLING

Since half the world are sellers and the other half buyers, it stands to reason that a great percentage of your staff are sellers. Whether your frontline sellers *(your real estate agents, car salespeople, pharmaceutical representatives, office receptionists, computer equipment trainers, waiters and maître d's and everyone in between)* are your ambassadors or your assassins depends considerably on how well they have mastered the art of selling. No matter what is to be sold, whether it is product or service, the goal is to provide a beneficial solution for the customer.

> *Most salesmen try to take 'the horse to water and make him drink'. Your job is to make the horse thirsty.*
>
> Gabriel M. Siegel, President
> MediCab of New York, Inc.
> (Speech to sales reps)

Successful selling takes two premises for granted—*first* that the seller understands the value of their product or service, AND *second*, that they understand their customers, their needs, expectations, concerns and problems. The onus is on the seller to accept this responsibility and satisfy both assumptions.

Use the following selling suggestions. Pass them on to your frontline staff. They work.

1. **Start with "C'mon in! It's good to see you."**

   Instead of beginning the conversation with "May I help you?" which invariably leads to an "I'm just looking" or "No thanks" response, welcome customers with a greeting that sounds as if you feel they're important and you're glad they came. It should sound much like your greeting to old friends when they come to visit.

   If you continue doing your paperwork, talking to other employees, or stocking your shelves, you can't look customers in the eye, smile and make appropriate sounds of welcome.

Customers long to feel wanted — liked — important. It makes them feel good. They are interested in remaining, and returning to where these feelings evolve. You can never go wrong treating customers as if they are VIPs.

Consider distance. In North America, personal space is highly valued and protected. Avoid approaching customers too quickly or too closely, as it can be perceived as threatening or confrontational. Wait until initial rapport is established. Once your customers feel at home, get ready to provide solutions.

Although the initial greeting step changes for "at home" selling, or appliance repair or trade show sales, or professional office visits, the objectives remain the same:

- *create a non-threatening, "glad you're here" environment.*

- *make customers feel good, maintain a high comfort level.*

- *demonstrate "you've got my undivided attention" with eye contact and a smile.*

Go beyond "May I help you?" to "How can I solve your problem?"

> *We all, in one way or another, send our little messages to the world.... And rarely do we send our messages consciously, we act out our state of being with non-verbal body language. We lift one eyebrow for relief. We rub our noses for puzzlement. We clasp our arms to isolate ourselves or to protect ourselves. We shrug our shoulders for indifference, wink one eye for intimacy, tap our fingers for impatience, slap our foreheads for forgetfulness....*
>
> Julius Fast, psychologist
> *Body Language*

2. Ask yourself, "Why, oh why do they buy?"

Find out. Observe. Very often customers give you a clue by asking about a specific product or service or by walking over to the area that is of interest. Ask open-ended questions *(ones that can't be answered by "yes" or "no")* such as: *"For what occasion(s) are you buying an outfit?"* or *"For whom did you want a live-in homemaker?"* *"Tell me something about her?"* or *"What are the dimensions of your bathroom?"* or *"What did you want to be able to do with your computer?"* or *"What direction does the area face that you are trying to landscape?"* It's difficult to come up with all the appropriate questions on the spur of the moment, so professional salespeople have a list of memorized and rehearsed questions on the tip of the tongue. The better the questions, the better the answers, *the better* you get to know your customers.

People avoid pain at all costs. If they are looking to replace or upgrade, one of the best questions to ask is what problems are being experienced with their current product or service and what they are looking to accomplish with the new product or service they want to purchase.

Learn to listen between the lines. Paraphrase what customers tell you while formulating questions that give you more information about their needs. The more accurately you pin-point customers' needs, the easier the sale will be.

The power of communication starts with the art of listening.

MAKE IT PAINLESS
- **Simplify the decision making process**
- **Organize the data into usable information**
- **Reduce complex verbiage into layman's language**
- **Minimize the risks/stress**
- **Consolidate information to avoid overload**
- **Inspire trust and confidence**

Sam Geist

Remember to ask affirming questions, such as, "If I understand you correctly, what you require is...." This type of questioning strengthens your rapport with your customers and confirms that you are on target.

Finally translate the customers' "needs information" into the products or services that will satisfy them. Offer alternatives if you haven't exactly what they want, clarifying how your product or service will also serve their needs.

3. **An expert knows. "This 'zxyograph' is truly amazing. It does everything in the house and...."**

In order to effectively, accurately match customers' needs to your products and services you must become an expert. Learn everything there is to know about everything you sell — manufacturing specifics, capabilities, shortcomings and most importantly how your products or services will satisfy the needs of each customer.

The FAB (Features.Attributes.Benefits) of product and service selling has been discussed on page 105 of Part Three on differentiating yourself. It warrants repeating here briefly, to emphasize how vital it is to stay tuned to WIFM.

Learn *the features* of your products and services. That is, all the things you can see, taste, touch, smell and hear.

Learn *the attributes* of your products and services. That is, what the features do.

Most importantly learn *the benefits* of your products and services. That is what the features and attributes do for your customers to satisfy their needs.

Customers don't buy features. They only buy what those features will do for them.

Customers are interested in benefits that will improve their lives. Dig deep for them.

Accumulate product and service knowledge. It is available from a variety of sources:

- *suppliers, manufacturers*
- *your own experience with the product/service*
- *other salespeople's experience with the product/service*
- *other customers', friends' experiences with the product/service*
- *industry research*

When you pass information on, acknowledge the source. It adds credibility.

Product and service credibility is further enhanced by the way the product is handled and service is described. Treat

This customer's plea says it well:
Don't sell me things,
Mr. Merchant.
Don't sell me clothes, sell me
neat appearance, style,
attractiveness.
Don't sell me shoes, sell me
foot comfort and the pleasure
of walking in the open air.
Don't sell me food, sell me
happiness and the pleasure
of taste.
Don't sell me plows, sell me
golden fields of waving wheat.
Don't sell me things, sell me
ideals, feelings, self-respect,
home life, happiness.
Please don't sell me things.

each product as if it were an irreplaceable diamond bracelet. Treat each service as if it were the cure mankind has been looking for. Respect, care and benefit is transferred to the customer, who will appreciate its quality and value its purchase.

Remember question six on *"A Training Program Checklist"* on page 209. It asks, *"Does the program explain why customers buy? Does it teach staff how their attitudes, behavior, actions affect the buying decision and their customers' perception of quality?"* A positive answer is what it's all about.

Customers judge products and services through your subtle, and your not so subtle signals. Your demeanor enhances not only the product, but your business' image as well. It certainly increases the opportunity for a sale, and a satisfied repeat customer.

4. **It's in the script: "A new lawn will certainly enhance the value of your property, and an underwater sprinkler system will ensure it stays as green and thick as the day it was professionally laid."**

   OR

   "Not only does the suit look custom-made on you, but I've got the perfect tie to complete the outfit."

When professionally practiced, "add-on" or suggestion selling benefits both customer and organization. Since, as the expert, you know the products you are selling or services you are providing *best*, you are able to enhance the purchase by making suggestions that will improve performance, increase ease of use and value. The benefit to the organization is two-fold. The salesperson has their professional role re-affirmed and the company has its bottomline profitability increased.

An interesting study bears this out. In its 1994 survey, the P.O.P. (Point of Purchase) Institute determined that for every dollar spent in a store, customers would have spent another dollar, had they been asked or encouraged to do so!

Today's customers want value. As a salesperson your responsibility lies not only in showing the best, but explaining the difference between best and good or better. Since the best generally performs at the highest level, it is to everyone's advantage, to sell at this level. It virtually assures customer satisfaction.

My son Michael and his wife Allison are proud of their new coffee maker. They were looking for something inexpensive, since they, themselves, don't drink coffee — this purchase was for guests. The salesperson at Macy's explained the features and benefits of various models, working up to the Porsche of coffee makers, a Krups with buttons for hotter, for stronger, for better. That's what they bought. If the differences hadn't been explained, they would have purchased a $19.95 coffee maker.

5. Ask: "Will that be cash or charge?"

It's one of the either/or ways to close a sale. Others include: "Do you want it delivered or will you take it with you?" "Do you want the green shirt or the blue shirt?" "Which is better, morning or afternoon delivery? What day do you prefer?" This type of close works well because the questions require positive responses.

When customers give clear buying signals whether they be verbal or action, it may be appropriate to assume the sale by walking over to the cash register or opening the order book. At this point, it is also helpful to suggest an additional item. You might comment to the customer that, "A five year service contract is available and is an excellent worry free investment," or "A new shipment of designer mugs just came in, that would be perfect with the cappuccino maker," or "In addition to regular pool maintenance, we sell pool chemicals and pool paraphernalia." The choice hastens the close with either "Yes include the mugs," or "No, I'll just take the cappuccino maker." In any case, the sale is made satisfactorily.

Don't lose a sale by missing discreet buying signals. Stay tuned to your customer. Don't talk yourself out of a sale by talking too much.

Even though the sale may take a long time to consummate, when it is concluded, all customers want the actual transaction completed quickly. Be organized. Demonstrate efficiency and speed while still taking the time to look the customer in the eye and thank them. These final moments offer a special opportunity to make a positive lasting impression to retain memorability and remain top-of-mind. It takes only a second to show appreciation for the sale.

6. **Greet repeat customers with, "It's so good to see you again."**

Building relationships, maintaining them and encouraging repeat business requires on-going, never-ending, consistent effort.

Add your own suggestions to these ideas to build, maintain and grow relationships.

- *Use their names whenever you talk to customers.*

- *Develop an active database and use it to keep customer information up-to-date.*

- *Stay in touch. Send postcards, newsletters, letters.*

- *Call customers a few days after they've made a major purchase and ask about their satisfaction. This one call alone has awesome value. Never try to sell anything during this call.*

- *Contact some customers every day. Collect information from them, just as you give information to them.*

Add some ideas of your own:

- _____

- _____

- _____

- _____

The value of loyal customers can not be underestimated. Research has shown that not only do they shop more frequently at your store, but they also spend more when they shop. Remember these top 20 percent of your customers will give you 80 percent of your business.

7. **Always conclude with "Thanks for coming in," or, "Thanks for giving us the opportunity to quote."**

"If you need any additional information, don't hesitate to call." But don't wait to see if they do.

Follow up! Follow up! Follow up!

Very often, customers need to be gently prodded, reminded that their problem is still not solved and you have just the solution. Following up makes good business sense; it reminds customers that you are there. Very often, in their busy lives, they forget.

Every fall, just before it turns cold, the representative from Magic Sweeps chimney cleaning company calls me to ask if I want my fireplace chimney cleaned out. Very often a year goes by without my using the fireplace, so I don't need the services. He still calls the next year, and the next, and when ever I do have my fireplace cleaned, Magic Sweeps is the company that does it.

This spring, I needed to re-sod my front lawn. I called four different companies. They all made appointments to come and give an estimate. One never showed up. The other three looked and estimated. As a matter of fact, one company provided a two-page description of its services *(in duplicate)* methodically separating out all costs. It took Wayne, the lawn estimator, about 30 minutes, sitting in his truck to do it.

Not one called me back to ask if I had any questions, or to see if I had decided what to do, or was there anything else I needed. *Not one.* Each of the companies had sent someone over *(one company sent two guys)*, had spent their time, had given their advice, but didn't follow up. Why? *(Is "follow up" on your checklist?)*

The quality of selling has deteriorated to the point that it takes little to be better than everyone else. Ask yourself and get staff to ask themselves these seven questions. Make the changes necessary in your selling environment, so that the answer is always yes!!

1. **Is there passion and energy in your office, plant, store? Do you exude it? Do your staff exude it?**

2. **Are staff trained so they know their customers and their customers' businesses well? Can they spot sales opportunities and service problems? Do they?**

3. **Is everyone in your organization part of the "selling and serving customers" process?**

4. **Do you, as the boss, inspire? Do you visibly lead the pack? Do you call customers regularly? Lead training**

sessions? Clearly communicate your commitment and interest to both staff and customers?

5. Do salespeople and other staff get both short and long-term recognition?

6. Does your organization take advantage of today's technology, utilize high tech equipment to ensure high touch—to ensure that the selling process is smooth, simple and effective?

7. Do you and your staff talk to customers frequently? Do you recognize customers' need for attention, for closer communication?

Interaction on an international scale begs additional questions:

Do you and your staff understand the customs, the traditions important to customers half way around the globe?

In his first effort to export to Japan, my brother-in-law made the mistake of bringing documents, agreements, attorneys to the first meeting. The Japanese were turned off. They had wanted to find out about John, about loyalty, about the heart. He learned from his experience and gives this advice to others. "To deal with Japanese organizations, leave your order sheets and price lists behind. Go to meet, to improve the relationship. When you get back home, the orders will follow by fax."

Finally, I am reminded of the poignant plea made by a frontliner during a training session I conducted for her company. She asked that management "not treat me as 'just' an employee, disinterested, just putting in time, just doing my job. Treat me as a partner, an associate, an ally ready to help you grow, ready to build your business. And that's just what I'll do!!"

"Why should someone do business with you...rather than someone else?"

ASK. ANSWER. PLAN. CHANGE.

Ask and answer these 21 questions to ensure your frontline = your bottomline.

1. **Why should someone do business with you...rather than someone else?**

   Why should someone work for you...rather than someone else?

   _____
   _____
   _____
   _____

2. **Is your hiring record effective? Why/why not?**

   _____
   _____
   _____
   _____

3. What can you change in the procedure, what can you include to ensure you hire ambassador types?

_____

_____

_____

_____

4. What do your employees want and need?
   How can you find out?

_____

_____

_____

5. Are you providing their wants and needs? How well?
   What can you do to improve?

_____

_____

_____

6. What motivators do you provide staff in your business environment?

_____

_____

_____

_____

7. What motivators can you add to the list?

    _____

    _____

    _____

    _____

    _____

8. Where can you get inspiration for additional
    motivators? Have you asked your staff for ideas?

    _____

    _____

    _____

    _____

    _____

9. What do you do to recognize and reward staff?

    _____

    _____

    _____

    _____

10. What else can you easily do?

    _____

    _____

    _____

    _____

11. Is your training program organized on a project or a process basis?

_____

_____

_____

_____

12. On a scale of one to 10, how would you rate the effectiveness of your training program?

_____

_____

_____

_____

13. List at least five ways it can be improved.

_____

_____

_____

_____

_____

14. What can you do to incorporate your ideas into your training program? Make a list. Create a plan.

_____

_____

_____

_____

15. How regularly do you hold joint staff/management
    meetings to solicit ideas and to air grievances?

    _____

    _____

    _____

    _____

16. Do the meetings enhance the atmosphere in your
    business? Why? Why not? What can you do to
    ensure they do?

    _____

    _____

    _____

    _____

    _____

    _____

17. Do you provide staff with evaluation of their
    performance on a regular basis? Do you provide
    your management team with evaluation of their
    performance on a regular basis?

    _____

    _____

    _____

    _____

    _____

18. What evaluation techniques do you use? List them.

_____

_____

_____

_____

_____

19. How can your evaluations be improved to further enhance staff satisfaction and productivity?

_____

_____

_____

_____

_____

20. What steps have you taken to empower staff? What additional steps can you take?

_____

_____

_____

_____

_____

21. How high are the brick walls of miscommunication in your business? What are you doing to knock them down? What else can you do?

_____

_____

_____

_____

Write in one additional question you feel is important to you, your situation as a result of reading this section — *and then answer it.*

Q. _____

_____

_____

_____

_____

_____

A. _____

_____

_____

_____

_____

_____

Part six moves the question *"Why should someone do business with you...rather than someone else?"* out of the marketplace environment, away from your customers' perspective, your marketing and service strategies and the responsibilities of your frontline — directly to you. It raises questions that require consideration, analysis and action. It outlines the requisites of a vision statement, its strategies and objectives, including suggestions for successful implementation. A perspective on re-engineering for growth is also espoused for consideration.

FROM VISION TO IMPLEMENTATION

6

Who are you?

Who do you want to be?

Where do you want to go?

How do you plan to get there?

Why should someone do business with you as you move toward your goal?

Why should they do business with you when you get there?

Vision — *flashes of image, undercurrents of memory, waves of optimism and hope* — begins as an unsettling desire to change, to capitalize on emerging opportunities, to take the future in hand. It grows, it blossoms into a bright, bold view of "all that can be."

> **Where there is no vision, the people perish.**
> Old Testament, Proverbs 29-18

Keep in mind that vision is not a strategy, nor is it operating plans. It is the beginning, the artist's rendering, designed to fascinate and involve. It is the creator's picture of a realistic, credible, attractive future for their organization — a powerful vision that moves everyone who comes in contact with it. It must be clearly defined, memorable, passionate! It must be innovative, differentiating, synergistic, farsighted. It must be an integral part of your personal needs and values, those of your organization, those of your customers.

In order for it to survive — to grow — to become implementable, your vision must develop tangible, communicable components, to guide you and your organization forward to a better tomorrow. It may be a difficult stretch, but it must be achievable. To be supported, it can't be mission impossible.

> *Everything depends on execution, having just a vision is no solution.*
> Stephen Sondheim, composer

With a vision, your strategies become deliberate, proactive, clear pathways to well-defined goals—your plans, your objectives are actualized. Without an implementation plan, your vision remains nothing but an ethereal dream. Conversely, without a vision, your plans and strategies lack focus. They lack purpose.

Start by asking yourself and your staff:

"Who are we?"

"How do we envision our organization's future?"

"Does our vision fit in with our vision of the marketplace around us?"

"What steps must we take to turn our vision into reality?"

Continue by asking, and answering questions such as these:

1. **Where have you, where has your organization been?**
    What is your history?

2. **What are your organization's strengths and weaknesses, needs, challenges and capabilities?**

3. **What has given you the greatest joy, the most difficulties in your organization?**

4. **What do you personally want to achieve?**
    What is important to you?

5. **What would you like to change most in your organization?**

6. **How will environmental factors — competitors, economy, technology, alliances — affect your vision?**

7. **What is driving your organization's agenda?**

8. **Do you have an understanding of how your field/industry will be different 10 years from now?**

9. **Who will benefit from your vision?**

10. **Have you put your vision in writing?**

11. **Is it a living frame of reference? A guide?**

> *Good questions are better than good answers.*
>
> David K. Hurst, management writer
> *Crisis & Renewal: Meeting the Challenge of Organizational Change*

12. **Have you discussed, shared, talked about your vision with staff, with business associates, with family, with friends?**

13. **What is the response of those around you?**

14. **Have you made assumptions based on your vision to see if it holds water?**

15. **Is everything you do — sales, marketing, production, administration, operations, customer service — in alignment with your vision?**

16. **Are technological trends in alignment with your vision? Which trends can enhance your vision?**

17. **Have you checked out your competitors' direction and strengths to ensure you are differentiating your vision?**

18. **Have you tested your vision?**

19. **Has it the flexibility needed in face of changing marketplace conditions?**

20. **How are you planning to implement it?**

21. **What are you doing to assess its congruency with your strategies?**

The questions provoke thought. The answers provide direction. They give focus. They provide the stepping stones to move your organization forward.

A VISION STATEMENT

"Tangibilizing" your vision with a vision statement gives it legs. Work together with your staff to develop a carefully formulated statement of intentions, one that clearly defines your destination — one that highlights where you and your organization want to be. An amazing transformation occurs when people who are to be the vision's implementers are also its architects. Everyone involved ends up "walking the talk." Everyone becomes part of the vision.

Your vision statement should be short — no more than 50 words — so that it will be remembered. Without referring to it, you and your staff should be able to recite it with almost complete accuracy. If it can't be remembered, how can it possibly be applied in all strategies, to all situations? It should feature the values and the guiding principles that hold your organization together. It must be future-oriented, indicating what the organization will be. And finally, it must specify a point in time: a three-to-five year time frame is often used.

Put your vision statement to the test for clarity of content.

- **Is its message clear?**
- **Do staff understand it?**
- **Can they explain what it means?**

- Does it create an organizational framework that is compelling, specific in intention, action-oriented?

Put your vision statement to the test for conformity to circumstances

- Does it "fit" your organization?
- Does it "fit" your strategies and the actions that will be required to be taken in the future, rather than what worked in the past?
- Is it flexible in the face of necessary strategic changes?

Put your vision statement to the test for credibility

- Is it believable? Do-able?
- Do the goals it anticipates parallel what is really happening?

An outmoded, inaccurate, longwinded vision statement is dangerous to the organization since it confuses strategic action and derails goals.

A client of mine developed this vision statement to guide his company to the future.

Vision 1997

"We will be the industry leader, utilizing research and development of our professional staff to introduce new, innovative waste-management solutions, based on environmental concerns, through a strategic alliance with global partners."

It has kept him on track and his organization growing.

Each of the key elements of his vision statement directed him toward strategic processes that were defined and undertaken. Once outlined, these strategies became the vehicles for his intent, his organization's intent to everyone inside and outside.

He solidified his strategies by attaching SMART objectives *(Specific, Measurable, Attainable, Realistic, Time-determined)* to them. He made his strategies achievable by assigning specific measurements that encouraged action.

His vision *to be the industry leader* directed him to strategically focus on attaining profitability, providing a good investment, achieving global recognition, developing an innovative stance and so on. His objective was to achieve revenues of $$ million by December 31, 1996.

His vision regarding *utilizing research and development of a professional staff* directed him to strategically focus on maintaining state-of-the-art research facilities, on providing professional development opportunities and on concentrating on technological advancement. His objective was to produce and market a cost efficient prototype of his technology and see hundreds of them installed in North America by January 1, 1998.

His vision regarding the *introduction of new innovative waste-management solutions* directed him to strategically focus on intensive research to develop a new solution to old problems. His objective was to develop waste-reduction equipment that reduced waste to 10 percent of its original volume by the end of 1996.

His vision regarding *environmental concerns* directed him to strategically focus on developing non-toxic, no emissions solutions. His objective was to refine his prototype to be toxic-free, emissions-free at time of installation, January 1, 1998.

Finally his vision regarding *a strategic alliance with global partners* directed him to strategically focus on finding and developing beneficial relationships with well-respected organizations from around the world. His objective was to finalize the relationships for global parts manufacturing and North American distributorship by January, 1997.

Each of his strategic components was clearly defined and a SMART objective was attached to provide a specific timed framework for achievement.

Another client developed the following vision statement several years ago together with her senior executives.

Vision Statement 1995

"We shall be the premier franchisor and specialty retailer of high-quality equipment and services dedicated to enhancing our customers' enjoyment of our product, better than any other provider.

We are committed to achieving superior results for shareholders within a culture that promotes trust, win/win relationships for all parties."

VISION STATEMENT 1995

ELEMENT	STRATEGIES	OBJECTIVES
1. premier franchisor & specialty retailer	- attract superior franchisees - develop specific areas of specialization	- open 150 franchised locations by Dec. 1995
2. high quality equipment	- re-merchandise with superior merchandise - provide "value added" services to customers - use high quality as a differentiating factor	- 80 percent of core merchandise & services in high end niche
3. better enhance our customers' enjoyment of product	- franchisee training - staff training - monitor competitors	- feature clinics every Saturday - offer advantage customer cards
4. superior results for shareholders	- keep shareholders informed - meet with shareholders	- increase stock value 20 percent by Dec. 1995
5. trust, win/win culture	- work as partners with staff - involve suppliers in partnership culture	- reduce employee turnover by 15 percent each year - increase customer retention to 90 percent by Dec. 1995

This vision statement provided the organization with a framework that assisted it to grow quickly in a short period of time. Each element of the statement directed the organization towards defining strategies to realize the vision — and to clarify the intent for others in the organization. Each strategy was solidified by attaching SMART objectives to it. All elements were indicated on a chart located in the boardroom and was available for discussion and reinforcement.

The combination of vision statement, strategic elements and vision objectives offers a clear, action-oriented approach. In its simplicity lies its power to establish, communicate and implement your organization's vision.

Move the vision toward implementation by steering it horizontally *(rather than vertically)* along the assembly line. Horizontal management is reshaping corporations, by organizing them around their essential processes — *production, manufacturing, sales, order fulfillment, service.* It assures problems are identified quicker, remedied easier and customer satisfaction is at the forefront of decision making. The vertical hierarchy is flattened and profitability is enhanced by eliminating components that add no value. Corporations are re-structured based on value to the organization — value to the customers.

Sophisticated information systems such as international computer networking are often the visionary linchpins that hold horizontal corporations together.

AT&T installed Fastar *(a computerized detection system of downed lines)* enabling it to restore customer service in 10 minutes as opposed to the 11 hours it took three years earlier. The appreciable reduction in time was accompanied by an equally large decrease in irate customer complaints.

Federal Express installed leading-edge computerization enabling both FedEx and its customers to quickly and accurately track deliveries. When I recently FedEx'ed an important package to a client, I was able to track it on the Internet. I knew exactly where it was at any given point in time and precisely when it arrived, making me feel completely informed and in control.

Visionary corporations assemble dream teams to ensure that the process priority focuses on customer satisfaction. Hallmark Cards used this team approach to cut across creative, manufacturing, production and distribution sectors to reduce completion time of its Shoebox cards from nine months to three. Gordon Fraser, a greeting card manufacturer in Britain did the same. Its "mad cow disease" cards hit the shelves scarcely six weeks after mad cow disease hit the headlines.

At Southwest Airlines, "visionizing" is conducted on a grand scale by Herb Kelleher, founder and CEO. His driving force is to ensure that his 13,000 employees and his customers are having a good time. Processes are geared to ensure that his vision becomes reality.

Kelleher takes a relaxed approach with his staff, encouraging communication. He knows most by name. Meetings often turn into parties because he feels that the unity that's required to make an organization work comes from sharing a variety of activities and experiences.

Kelleher takes a focused approach to the business of profit and loss. Southwest operates on providing a combination of short and cheap runs. Most runs last about an hour at under under $100 for a one way ticket. Its successful short-haul charter concept remains unchanged.

On a small scale, Betty Draper, a retailer from New Jersey, saved her upscale women's wear shop from certain demise by recognizing her problems and deciding who she wanted to become.

She envisioned her retail business as a fun workplace, marked by effective communication and problem solving, innovatively run and merchandised— *profitable*.

She realized in order to achieve these goals, there were strategies she would need to develop and outline, challenges she would have to address.

She met with her staff of 20 and outlined her vision and her strategies. All those who felt they were unable to share this vision were replaced by staff who were committed to the company and Draper's vision of the future. However, she forged ahead too quickly, hiring new staff, giving them carte blanche and watched as her goals faded into the distance.

She re-examined her situation and with external assistance and advice, reorganized her agenda to include regular avenues to share, to review, to plan, to report, to assess and to re-new. She slowed changes down to the pace that both she and her staff could handle and effectively respond. Draper instituted a training program to enhance the skills of new staff, a sales training program to upgrade skills of existing staff and disseminated new management techniques in order to be able to promote from within. The organization began to change.

In the two years since its inception, her vision led toward the development of a fun work environment where the positive is embraced and celebrated and the negative is discussed for correction and improvement—where professional, trained staff are comfortable and secure in their roles to offer customers the products and services they want.

A final note. Customers are delighted with the attention, the "value-added" they receive. Sales are up and both staff and Betty Draper are smiling.

In small business there are no small mistakes.

Retailers in Fortune

"Visionizing", its plans, strategies and objectives require:

- *strong, focused, bold leadership*

- *good interrelationships and communication. (For example, staff need to know why their jobs are changing)*

- *an internal retraining and reward system*

- *determined focus on customer needs, utilizing customer-driven research to improve the organization again and again*

Doesn't all successful management have those same requirements?

James Collins, a management consultant, pointed out that visionary organizations have more than a vision, no matter how driving, to guide them through today's marketplace; they hold core ideologies that they preserve with religious zeal. Even as they adapt to changing times, their corporate culture remains intact because it defines the character of the organization. Their core ideology embodies their guiding principles and beliefs as well as their raison d'être. Think Hewlett-Packard *(respect for individual, commitment to quality, community responsibility)*, think Dofasco *("Our product is steel, our strength is people")*, think Nordstrom *(unconditional customer service)*, think The Walt Disney World Company *(imagination and wholesomeness)*.

> ### *Good thoughts are no better than good dreams, unless they are executed!*
> Ralph Waldo Emerson, (1803-1882),
> American essayist and poet
> *Nature*

There are organizations who appear to change dramatically, but it is their operating practices or their business strategies that are revised—not their core values and purpose—*they remain constant.*

RE-ENGINEERING FOR GROWTH

When you travel from "visionizing" to implementation, you will undoubtedly bump into an assortment of management strategies, each with its advocates and its naysayers! Critics of each strategy from Total Quality Management (TQM) to Re-engineering to Open Book Management can offer up evidence of great successes—and great failures.

All too often corporations looking for a lifeline, grab whatever strategy they can manage to snag as they career, rudderless, downstream. Without examining the strategy's tenets carefully, without determining its appropriateness to *their situation*, they use the most popular "fishing tackle" of the time. Sometimes it works. Sometimes it doesn't.

Strategies must be scrutinized against the whole of the organization, not just the injurious parts. They must be considered not only for the short term, but for the long term. They must be objectively appraised against the losses that may be incurred as well as the advantages to be gained.

Re-engineering, for example, was orchestrated and implemented to help organizations face the challenges of the

1990s. Unfortunately the growth factor went missing from the strategy and re-engineering became a surgical procedure that permitted those in control to cut away the core culture of the organization, anesthetize its values, lose its leaders, its role models, its workers, and mistake corporate knowledge for an appendix or a gall bladder and discard it. The goals of this re-engineering procedure were intended to:

- *increase productivity*

- *optimize value to shareholders*

- *decrease operating costs*

- *improve utilization of resources by the elimination of unnecessary levels and jobs.*

It generally succeeded in achieving most of these goals—but at what costs! As a post-op side effect, re-engineering left many of the corporations bleeding profusely. Had the "growth" element been attached to re-engineering, hemorrhaging would, in many cases, have been prevented and the organization not suffered.

Strategies to accommodate change have been offered up fast and furious in the last few years. Many initially appeared as beneficial trends, only to be found out as flash-in-the-pan fads. Trendy strategies satisfy only temporarily.

In two studies recently conducted, research indicated that satisfaction with those strategies never surpassed 60 percent

(10 to 40 percent satisfaction in Gibson & Co. study; 35 to 60 percent satisfaction in Electric Power Research Institute Study).

To stay healthy, to prosper over the long term organizations need to grow. Growth strengthens staff morale and productivity. It encourages momentum. It rewards investors. From 1988 to 1994 in the United States, the compound annual growth rate in the market value of organizations that increased revenue *and* profits was 19 percent. During that same time, the growth rate for organizations that increased profits *(presumably by cutting costs/downsizing)* more rapidly than they increased revenue was 12 percent, as outlined in *Grow to be Great: Breaking the Downsizing Cycle*, co-authored by Dwight Gertz and Joao P. A. Baptista.

Whether its called restructuring or reframing or revitalization or renewal, its goal must be growth. As a perspective toward growth, the strategy becomes a positive process that beneficially alters the landscape of the corporation for its good — the good of staff — the good of customers. Downsizing is not a viable long term business strategy. You can't shrink to greatness! You have to grow!!

Both Eastman Kodak and Bausch & Lomb were looking to grow. Both succeeded because they acknowledged the value of their core businesses, their core competencies and developed opportunities based on what they did best. Kodak refocused on the business that made it great—*photography*—by seizing the opportunity the advent of digital photography afforded it. Bausch & Lomb shed its unprofitable operations and found strength by building its core business—contact lenses, lens-care products and Ray Ban sunglasses. It grew each of these areas into a dominating global market presence.

To survive and grow in the 21st Century, organizations must re-invent themselves — re-structure themselves. Use a re-engineering for growth platform and prepare an effective, productive, profitable strategic plan. It takes the bold shared vision of the leader. It takes a planned approach, a clear mandate, and an organizational operation that is consistent with the vision. It takes the support and trust of the team. It takes recognizing the need for staff to be able to function in their new environment, by educating and empowering them to do their new job.

The will to win is important, but the will to prepare is vital.

Joe Paterno, football coach
Penn State University
American Heritage

Re-engineering for growth offers solid benefits and advantages. It revitalizes and renews you, your organization, your staff. It assists you, your organization, your staff become more profitable, more competitive.

- *It increases staff interest and involvement in the organization.*

- *It increases staff knowledge, achievements, competencies, sense of ownership.*

- *It improves internal communication, co-operation and realization of diverse needs.*

- *It improves matching of skills and empowerment to responsibilities and processes.*

- *It improves alignment of performance to marketplace needs and demands.*

Formulate your re-engineering for growth platform by setting goals based on a vision for growth; by developing innovative processes that create and sustain growth; by benchmarking to raise the bar; by encouraging and rewarding change and transformation; by monitoring, assessing and refining the re-engineering for growth processes.

The opportunity to re-engineer for growth is everywhere. Research shows that two out of every three U.S. companies laying off staff are simultaneously hiring new staff for other departments. AT&T, vilified for their layoffs, hired in other areas so the size of their workforce was not decreased. They're training where necessary and adding staff where needed. They're learning to do more with less, by re-organizing the work processes more efficiently, by utilizing horizontal management. Here are just a few of a growing list of organizations who are succeeding at re-engineering themselves for growth. They have used a solid

> *They're [U.S. companies] getting rid of everything that fails to give them a competitive advantage and they're expanding areas that add value.*
>
> Eric Rolfe Greenberg, director of management studies
> American Management Association

strategy, implemented by visionary management and backed by courageous staff. Read, adapt and implement.

Gillette re-invented itself when it re-invented shaving. Its growth has been phenomenal since its introduction of the Sensor, a new product to its old market.

> *Good products come out of market research. Great products come from R & D.*
>
> Alfred Zeien, CEO
> Gillette
> *Fortune*

Over the past five years, more than 40 percent of Gillette sales have come from new products, helping to pump up stock price, to the delight of investors. Only new products that represent significant improvements are brought to market. Anchored by a strong technological base, Gillette is No. 1 worldwide in its markets–profitable and fast growing. By offering new, improved products, to an existing market, you grow.

Staples re-invented itself when it re-invented the selling and delivery of business supplies. Its product did not change, but its merchandising, distribution and pricing structure certainly did. By pioneering a new retail format, you grow.

Sears re-invented itself when it re-invented its shoe business. Its customers considered it a family apparel store and as such expected to be satisfactorily outfitted from head to toe. Customers were unhappy about shortages in shoe styles and sizes. Sears goal was to improve its shoe business by ensuring it had the right merchandise at the right time in the right size in its stores. In this way, it would be able to fulfill its customers' expectations that they could count on Sears for all their family's footwear needs. Sears envisioned a distribution system that was technologically a competitive advantage, one that would enable it to solve problems of overstocks, undershipping and inaccurate shipping. Problems that prevented Sears from fulfilling its promise.

You've got to think about "big things" while you're doing small things, so that all the small things go in the right direction.

Alvin Toffler, futurist & writer
Newsweek

The strategic plan included construction of a state-of-the-art automated footwear distribution center where employees ride wire-guarded lift trucks, instead of pushing carts. To collect bar coded merchandise, staff are guided by light trees that flash to indicate which styles and quantities are to be picked. This process realizes two advantageous developments. Two hundred and fifty pairs of shoes, instead of 70 pairs, can be picked by each employee in an hour and merchandise replenishment is accomplished in four days rather than two weeks. By using advanced technology to get the right merchandise to the right place at the right time, you grow.

Procter & Gamble faced the monumental task of re-engineering for growth, as reported in *Fortune* magazine, and is succeeding, based on a two-pronged approach—better value and new markets philosophy. Its goal

The hardest thing for a company is to change its thinking.

Edwin Artzt, former CEO
Procter & Gamble
Fortune

in re-designing its product development, its manufacturing processes, its distribution channels, its pricing strategies, its markets and products, was to deliver better value at every point along the supply chain. P&G knew they had to link supplier, wholesaler, retailer and consumer into a continuous loop. At the same time it had to re-think its pricing strategy to make it competitive in today's marketplace. Its commitment to everyday low prices presupposed it maintained everyday low costs. It had to change almost everything it did—*and fast*.

Procter & Gamble's four rules for change:
1. *change the work*
2. *do more with less*
3. *eliminate rework*
4. *reduce costs that can't be passed on to the consumer.*

Products were ordered, replenished, billed and paid for electronically, using "the loop" approach—minimizing errors, decreasing out-of-stocks and improving cash flow. Inventory was scrutinized in a matter of hours rather than weeks. Marketing promotions were minimized, and as a result, prices were kept competitive with private store brands.

Procter & Gamble went further. It standardized its product sizes thereby reducing the number of size configurations available, and eliminating 25 percent of its SKUs *(stock keeping units)*. This product strategy was appreciated by retailers and Procter & Gamble financial analysts alike.

Marketing strategy was revised to take advantage of the "hub & spoke" theory, abandoning the previous marketing "line" theory. It proved to be much more efficient, and more cost-effective to add new versions *("spokes")* to the original product *("hub")*, than to introduce a new product with a new name that was actually based on an existing product.

Both Tide and Crest provide excellent examples of the "hub & spoke" theory, with original Tide and Crest as the hubs and the versions such as Tide With Bleach, Super Concentrated Tide and Crest with Tarter fighting ingredients as the spokes.

Procter & Gamble is actively searching for more markets and more products. Aware that interest in health care will grow tremendously in the next millennium, they are involved in expanding that segment of the market by developing new and better products to match the marketplace's demand for younger, slimmer, brighter.

To successfully implement its global aspirations, Procter & Gamble realized that existing product versions require modifications in order to be positively received around the world. Many countries may want American products, exactly as they are, but are unable to afford them. For markets such as Brazil, Procter & Gamble created products like Pampers Uni, a less expensive version of Pampers. Featuring both versions on store shelves has been found to encourage trading up. For markets like Asia, where only seven percent of diapers are disposable, the opportunity for growth is unimaginable. By improving almost everything you do, you grow.

Other success stories include AlliedSignal, whose CEO, Larry Bossidy is a staunch advocate of re-engineering for growth. He focuses his efforts toward developing new targets for growth— toward finding new ways to grow.

Larry Bossidy's prescription for growth, outlined in *Fortune* magazine, has been re-echoed by many 1990s business consultants:

- *Cut the fat — be efficient! Only the lean are able to grow and be profitable.*

- *Set killer goals — stretch! Motivate! Visualize hard to get goals into focus.*

- *Grow through globalization. New markets, like China and India, are always emerging. Be a futurist.*

- *Multiply new products — be innovative! New — fresh — different — unique encourages growth.*

- *Make niche acquisitions — look for small splinters that will add key products and key services that you as yet don't have or provide.*

- *Claw your way to victory — push! Use your energy effectively. Set and meet growth goals. (Forget excuses: no one cares about them anyway!)*

There's no such thing as a mature market. What we need is mature executives who can find ways to grow.

Larry Bossidy, CEO
AlliedSignal
Fortune

By stretching your parameters, you grow.

Larry Bossidy could easily have added:

- *Re-frame your existing parameters — infuse new resolve — search for new vistas to stretch your borders.*

- *Re-structure your existing processes — tighten up ineffective, non-productive areas — become highly competitive.*

- *Revitalize your existing structure — encourage growth by linking the corporation to its surrounding environment.*

- *Re-new your vision and strengthen capability of staff — direct, infuse spirit, train. Enable staff to regenerate themselves and by so doing, regenerate your corporation.*

Their form of expression may differ but the sentiments of many of the CEOs examined were similar.

Responsible for its re-structuring, Jack Welch, CEO of GE *(General Electric)*, engaged in realistic self appraisal and then began to "delayer." He felt less was more. Managing less was managing better: fewer interpreters, fewer filters, fewer opportunities for miscommunication. He pushed productivity, he trimmed inventories, dismantled bureaucracies and attacked inefficiencies with a vengeance. He also surprised analysts by thrusting GE even deeper into services. In arenas such as health care and utilities, Welch sees GE's potential at providing sophisticated services that spring from its industrial strengths. By broadening the mix from manufacturing to include services, GE is

> ### *The secret to success is constancy to purpose.*
> Benjamin Disraeli, (1804-1881), British prime minister and novelist

re-shaping itself once again to maximize its anticipated potential and is expected to become America's most profitable company. It required analysis and action. By *doing it,* you grow.

His perspective reminded me of an admonition I repeat at every presentation I give. "Doing nothing is making a choice."

The choices we make during the "re-engineering for growth" process fuel us forward or stall us out.

Restructuring a company, re-engineering it for growth is an enormous task, irrevocably altering the complexion of the organization — and not always for the benefit of all. Procter & Gamble's improved efficiencies cost 13,000 jobs (12 percent of their workforce) worldwide.

Keep these 10 Do's in mind as you develop and implement *your* action plan **to 'Re-engineer for Growth'.**

1. Consider the plan's impact throughout the organization, not just in one or two areas.

   Ask: **Will re-engineering provide an immediate advantage? A long-term advantage? What is its cost?**

2. Question existing methodology. Develop new processes.

   Ask: **Is there a re-engineering model for us to use as a guide? Will the re-engineering process serve as a useful model for others?**

3. Develop a natural process order. Many processes need to be implemented on a concurrent, rather than in sequential order.

   Ask: **Will individual processes stand alone during re-engineering? Will they fit together again after re-engineering? Is re-engineering focused toward speed, simplicity, viability?**

4. View process results along a continuum, not as isolated events.

   Ask: **Is it measurable?**

5. Focus on the inherent value of the process for all concerned.

   Ask: **Who will benefit now? Who will benefit in the long term?**

6. Use resources and new technologies to maximize the positive results of the process and empower staff to do their jobs effectively.

   Ask: **Is everyone in the organization involved?**

7. Create teams by process, not departments.

   Ask: **Is everyone trained to do the job? Given the tools? Given the authority?**

One thing that makes one company better than another is ideas.

Don Bagin, publisher
Frank Grazian, executive director
Communication Briefings

8. Create realistic goals, assess them frequently and work conscientiously toward them.

    Ask: **Are there checks and balances incorporated into the plan?**

9. Don't procrastinate. Act.

    Ask: **When is the best time to begin?**

10. Assess—reassess—re-reassess.

    Ask: **Why should someone do business with me now? Why should someone do business with me when the process is completed?**

STRATEGY IMPLEMENTATION

The road from "visionizing" to implementation is long and winding, made all the more difficult by the presence of potholes—ineffective communication—lack-luster training—lack of foresight—inefficient use of resources—fuzzy focus.

An effective strategic plan with observation platforms along the way is an invaluable road map. It highlights dynamic route choices to THE DESTINATION. It presents options. It marks routes under construction. It includes expected travel times, speed limits. It indicates detours and attractions to be enjoyed along the way, together with their price of admission.

The great end of life is not knowledge but action.

Thomas Henry Huxley, (1825-1895), British biologist
Science and Culture

This road map offers you and your organization a multi-level perspective, much like a blueprint. It includes a market position perspective, a manufacturing perspective, a skills or resource perspective, an organizational development perspective, a staff training perspective, and a marketing perspective. It includes everything that is of particular importance to you and your organization. Develop and follow the multi-level plan that reflects your needs, your aspirations, your goals and those of your organization.

Some high schools now teach entrepreneurship to inculcate in their students the skills that generate excellence in the workforce. Teens learn to be determined, to initiate change, to develop a tolerance for risk taking, to think from both the strategic and creative sides of their heads. They are taught to initiate action, to demonstrate innovation, to exude self confidence, to accept success and failure and move with their knowledge.

Lynne Allen, Coordinator of Entrepreneurship Education for Ontario's Industry Ministry, who supervises one such entrepreneur program said, "These skills enable us to take advantage of change, not be victims of it. These are life-time skills you can apply in small business, large business or whatever you do."

The greatest thing in the world is not so much where we are, but in what direction we are moving.

Oliver Wendell Holmes, (1809-1894), American physician and writer
The Autocrat of the Breakfast Table

Ask questions that require deliberate contemplation and consideration. Questions such as:

- **What new core competencies, what pivotal capabilities to maintain a leadership position, will we need to build in order to implement the vision?**

- **What new product concepts or services will we need to pioneer?**

- **What alliances will we need to form?**

- **What existing programs should we protect?**

- **What long-term regulatory initiatives should we pursue?**

Difficult questions often go unanswered because they challenge top management—their foresight—the organization's future. Ask and answer them.

> *If we did all the things we were capable of doing, we would literally astonish ourselves.*
>
> Thomas Edison, (1847-1931)
> inventor

The list of questions is long. The information needed is sizable—obtaining the correct answers is vital. They will enable you to develop a strategy based on information *not* conjecture. ASK! Ask staff, ask customers, ask suppliers, ask friends. ASK.

Synthesize all information into a vision determining where the organization should go. Develop an appropriate, beneficial strategy which stands on firm ground, not quicksand.

Today it is beneficial for an organization to think of itself as a collection of evolving capabilities not just a collection of products and services, *(just as Jack Welch of GE has done)*. By realizing that evolution is part of the growth and changing process, the organization develops a flexible perspective that enables it to move in new directions.

> ***The key to achievement lies in being a "how" thinker, not an "if" thinker.***
>
> Anonymous

Start by asking what you can do—what you can change in your organization— what you can make better—how you can add value.

"Why should someone do business with you...rather than someone else?"

ASK. ANSWER. PLAN. CHANGE.

Start by asking and answering these 21 questions.

1. **Why should someone do business with you...rather than someone else? Why should someone do business with you next year—in five years? In 10 years?**

   _____

   _____

   _____

   _____

   _____

   _____

   _____

2. What is your vision for your company?
   What is your staff's vision?

_____
_____
_____
_____

3. Have you researched the viability of your vision?

_____
_____
_____

4. How will you ensure that customers are in alignment
   with your vision?

_____
_____
_____
_____

5. What is your vision statement?
   Have you written it down?

_____
_____
_____
_____

6. Have you put it to the test? Is its content appropriate? Does it fit your organization? Is it credible, believable? How will you ensure that everyone in all departments in your organization is aligned with your vision?

7. What strategies will you implement to make your vision reality?

8. Who will plan the strategies? Who will execute them?

9. What objectives will you strive to reach to make your vision reality? What innovative or breakthrough goals do you intend to achieve?

10. What value, what benefits do you envision your plan will have for your customers?

_____

_____

_____

_____

11. What value, what benefits do you envision your plan will have for you, your company, your staff?

_____

_____

_____

_____

12. What skills will be required to move from vision to implementation?

_____

_____

_____

_____

13. Who in the organization has those skills? What are your plans for acquiring skills not presently available in the organization?

_____

_____

_____

_____

14. What environmental factors affect your vision?

15. What competitive factors affect your vision?

16. What mechanisms are you including in your strategy to assess viability, progress and success along the way?

17. In determining the success of strategy, what percentage of your time is devoted to looking outside the organization to external issues, such as marketplace concerns and technological development?

18. In determining the success of the strategy, what percentage of your time is devoted to future-focusing?

_____

_____

_____

_____

_____

19. Is your vision in sync with today's rapid change?
With tomorrow's rapid change?
What can you do to ensure it is?

_____

_____

_____

_____

_____

20. What competitive advantages will the implementation of your vision give your organization?

_____

_____

_____

_____

_____

21. What new opportunities will the implementation of your vision give your organization?

_____

_____

_____

_____

Write in one additional question you feel is important to you, your situation as a result of reading this section — *and then answer it.*

Q. _____

_____

_____

_____

_____

_____

A. _____

_____

_____

_____

_____

_____

Part seven concludes the focus on leadership by outlining 25 characteristics and skills of successful leaders. Highlighted are the special gifts that truly enlightened leaders give their people, such as trust, empowerment, learning, respect and a supporting team environment, to enable everyone in the organization to answer *"Why should someone do business with you...rather than someone else?"*

A Catalyst for Action 7

Why should someone follow you?

Why should they want to work in an organization that has you as a leader?

Would you follow you? Would you want you as a leader? Why?

Horst Schulze, President and COO of The Ritz-Carlton defined the essence of leadership when he said, "Leadership to me is a very simple thing—creating consensus and aligning people behind a vision, not only telling people what needs to be done but—and this is key—*why it should be done*. Creating an environment in which people want to do the job, rather than have to do the job—that is leadership."

The principle role of leaders is to catalyze everyone in the organization so they, in turn, can catalyze each other. Leaders spread the light rather than bask in it, so the entire organization is illuminated, rather than only a small part of it.

LEADERS ARE MADE

> *Contrary to the opinion of many people, leaders are not born. Leaders are made, and they are made by effort and hard work.*
>
> Vince Lombardi, (1913-1970),
> Professional football coach
> *Lombardy,* Weibusch

Great leaders are visionaries, futurists, change-agents, confidantes, coaches, judges, role models, mentors, and guides. They lead, not merely manage. They open lines of communication to spread the word. They influence—direct—teach. They are secure enough to delegate. They develop their people skills, not only their process skills. They heed the principles, the beliefs and the values the rest of us believe in. They exemplify the integrity, the strength of character and the heroic demeanor that inspires action. They set the standard. They walk their talk.

They re-examine their actions. They re-evaluate their agenda, incorporating the latest statistics, the newest information both locally and globally, the changing marketplace's needs and demands, the competition's strategy. They re-create their plan based on new information. They re-write their agenda if necessary. They are flexible in the face of change realizing that nothing is carved in stone.

Leaders are their organizations' conductor, indicating directions to be taken, orchestrating the approach, while ensuring that their organization and its employees are playing from the same sheet music. They must encourage those around them to give outstanding performances while conducting from the sidelines so the light of staff achievement is their own.

Leaders must blend together the art, the music and the science of leadership with its psychology to motivate, to inspire and ensure they and their staff give unforgettable performances.

The fundamental characteristics, the essential requisites of outstanding leadership have not changed in more than 2,500 years.

Leaders grow into their role, as their appreciation and empathy for staff develops, as they demonstrate that appreciation and empathy.

Leaders prosper in their role as their knowledge of their organization's position in the marketplace expands, as they differentiate the organization from its competitors, as they adopt a customer perspective, as they define a niche and market to it.

Leaders succeed as they approach each day with renewed vision of their organization's possibilities and exemplify dedication to make it happen.

Leaders maintain their position when they ask and answer questions such as these:

1. **Am I facing reality? Seeing my organization the way it is? Locally? Globally?**

> *The superior leader gets things done with very little motion. He imparts instruction not through many words but through a few deeds. He keeps informed about everything but interferes hardly at all. He is a catalyst, and though things would not get done as well if he weren't there, when they succeed he takes no credit. And because he takes no credit, credit never leaves him.*
>
> Lao-Tzu (604 - 531 B.C.)
> Chinese philosopher and founder of Taoism
> *Tao Te Ching*

2. Am I acting on reality? Am I pro-active—acting quickly?

3. Do I know what my competitors are doing? Am I ahead? Do I know how to get ahead?

4. Am I changing in sync with the times? Am I encouraging my people to change with the times?

5. Do I know my people? Have I prepared them to act?

6. Do I know my customers? Have I created a vision that is in sync with their vision, their beliefs?

7. Am I doing what is good for the organization, staff, customers for the short-term? For the long-term?

8. Do I encourage dialogue? Do I listen well? Do I collect ideas?

9. Do I communicate effectively?

10. Do I underpromise and overdeliver?

VALUES AND VISION

There's no point running up a hill yelling "charge!" if no one is following you.

Gerald Greenwald, CEO
UAL Inc.
Fortune

Followers expect their leaders to possess impeccable character credentials. The "do as I say, not as I do" philosophy holds no water here. Your staff, your management group, your senior executives are with you because they respect your values and your beliefs. It is only through your words and your actions that they are able to see and judge your values and beliefs—*and they do!*

Keep your values and your vision consistent. Ensure your values are consistent with your vision. Values, vision, action must be in harmony. If they aren't, either change your vision, change what you value or change what you do.

That's just the rule Jere Ratcliffe, chief Scout executive of the 85-year-old Boy Scouts of America, followed. Ratcliffe's strategic benchmarking and team approach were well respected. He realized however that the Scouts needed a measurable corporate plan to determine that impact and effectiveness. He developed a plan to align the values held by the Scouts and their vision for future scouting in order to move the Boy Scout movement forward.

Whether it's a non-profit organization or a for profit conglomerate the need to align values, vision and action remains.

COMMUNICATE TO ENERGIZE

Gerald Greenwald, CEO of UAL Inc. (parent company of United Airlines), remarked in an interview with *Fortune* magazine (October 1996) that, "It is essential for leaders to communicate well with all staff and be able to justify all their actions to their staff." With evidence that trust of leadership is at an all time low, ensuring that your staff has confidence in you, is invaluable. Where there is no trust, there is no loyalty.

Max DePree, in his book *Leadership Jazz,* commented that, "At the core of being a leader is the need to connect one's voice and one's touch." Nowhere is this skill more essential than in communicating with staff. While every leader wants to feel he has the confidence of his employees, only the truly empathetic leaders are privy to their employees thoughts and words. Because the employee point-of-view and opinion is so valuable to decision making and because so much is risked to give it, it is the leader's duty to clear the paths of much needed communication and keep them open by both voice and touch.

For the most beneficial communication, nothing a leader can do, is more effective than listening. *Really listening.* It affords the opportunity to learn far more than you expected.

When Dennis Longstreet, was asked to head up Johnson & Johnson's Ortho Pharmaceutical subsidiary, he realized he would have to hire global talent— with intense commitment, flexibility and the ability to work as a team. A tough task! Utilizing such diverse individuals took organized communication. Said Longstreet: "It's about listening to people—their problems and their aspirations. It's amazing how unaware you can be of the impact you have on people different from you. It's very easy for people to start feeling excluded because of artificial barriers." Listening opens doors.

I still vividly recall the situation of Stephan, a client of my former advertising agency, who owned a chain of restaurants. For years, there had been only the most meager communication between him and his group of 40 franchisees. Most matters were handled by phone. Co-operation, morale, impetus to move the organization forward was in a sad state. Stephan insisted that our agreement included not only advertising and marketing service, but also organizing and facilitating regular franchisee/franchisor meetings.

You cannot manage men into battle. You manage things, you lead people.

Grace Murray Hopper, admiral (retired)
U.S. Navy
Nova

The first of these meetings created antagonism even before the selection of a suitable day, time and location could be decided. It was finally resolved to hold that meeting in a hotel, since it was neutral territory. After two hours of shouting and threats, the meeting was adjourned.

When positive, productive communication between leader and those they lead is not conducted, walls of misunderstanding sprout up. People need encouraging, interested leaders in order to assist them to develop their own potential, to enable them to voice their ideas, to air their grievances and to do "their own thing."

My definition of a leader...is a man who can persuade people to do what they don't want to do, or do what they're too lazy to do, and like it.

Harry S. Truman, (1884-1972),
Thirty-third President of the United States
More Plain Speaking, Miller

It took time. Regular meetings were held to inform franchisees of upcoming events and promotions. Their input was sought—and included. Brainstorming sessions became part of the agenda. Over an 18 month period, attitudes changed, frustrations were shared, hopes and aspirations grew, challenges were translated into new opportunities. And Stephan became, once again, regarded as a leader.

LEAD BY GIVING GIFTS

Good leaders give their staff small gifts—tickets to a ball game, a free lunch, a day off, a small treat. Great leaders give their staff big gifts—opportunity, space to grow and develop, exhilarating challenges, purpose to their work, trust, recognition and empowerment.

> *"A tale is told of a man in Paris during the upheaval in 1848, who saw a friend marching after a crowd toward the barricades. Warning him that the barricades could not be held against the troops, that he had better keep away, he received the reply, 'I must follow them, I am their leader.'"*

A. Lawrence Lowell, (1856-1943),
President, Harvard University

The value of giving big gifts is tremendous, yet many leaders are afraid to give them. Larry Sternberg of The Ritz-Carlton Tysons Corner crystalized this reluctance in *Turned On* by Roger Dow and Susan Cook. "When you strip away all the excuses for not empowering people, one thing remains: a lack of trust.

Either you feel that if you do not control these individuals with policies, rules, and inspections they are going to commit malfeasance or you do not trust that they have the necessary knowledge, experience and information to make a high-quality decision. The new role of a leader is to provide individuals and teams with that knowledge, experience, and information, then trust in them to make good decisions."

Give gifts worth giving. Make promises worth making. Your gifts are your commitments. Your staff believe them and expect them to be carried out. They will question you about them because your promises affect their very lives.

> **Ninety-five percent of American managers today say the right thing. Five percent actually do it.**
>
> James O'Toole, professor and leadership expert
> University of Southern California
> *Fortune*

What do you promise? What do you give?

In the case of Stephan, my franchisor-client whose goal was to create enough harmony to give him back his authority as the old king, he got much more. Effective communication eliminated his fear of giving the big gifts—*trust and empowerment*. By trusting his franchisees and empowering them with co-operative decision-making opportunities, he allowed them to accept more responsibilities. And they did. Empowering action-izes. It facilitates implementation. It powers up the people just as it powers up the leader.

A good friend of our family is a therapist whose practice

consists mostly of young singles. She finds the most frequent problem many of her clients face, is that they communicate with new acquaintances as if these acquaintances were just born, with no old memories or painful experiences. She reminds her clients that we often meet people in the middle chapters of their lives, without benefit of how their story unfolded. It takes much more sensitivity, more patience, more time to communicate well from an obstructed perspective.

Her remarks sent off a flare. I realized leaders labor under this handicap regularly. Good leaders overcome it by demonstrating more sensitivity, more patience, giving more time, seeing through a variety of lenses simultaneously— just as new friends must do.

> *You can't lead a cavalry charge, if you think you look funny on a horse.*
>
> John Peers, President
> Logical Machine Corporation
> *1,001 Logical Laws*

> *If you hire people smaller than you are, we shall become a company of dwarfs. If, on the other hand, you always hire people who are bigger than you are, we shall become a company of giants.*
>
> David Ogilvy, founder
> Ogilvy & Mather Advertising
> *Ogilvy on Advertising*

BE FEARLESS

As a catalyst, you must be fearless. A fear of flying necessitates long train trips. A fear of people who are smarter, bigger, better than yourself creates dwarfism in your organization.

Confident leaders understand this. They don't expect to solve all the organization's problems alone. They are secure enough in their vision and their strategies to delegate responsibility for the planning and the process along the line. They realize their role is to get things started and facilitate the plan.

As a catalyst, you must be fearless about the future. A fear of the future grinds the organization to a halt. Recognize that your challenges will be different in the future from what they are today. The solutions, therefore, must be different. As you ask leadership-type questions for today, ask them for tomorrow as well.

> *My major job is creating the next generation of leadership. Success to me in this company is not only getting a financially healthy and growing company again—it's also having arrived at the day that I can leave here and this place can run as well without me as it can with me.*
>
> George Fisher, Chairman
> Eastman Kodak
> *Forbes*

Questions like:

- **Who will our customers be tomorrow...in five years... in 10 years?**

- **What communication channels will we use to reach our customers in the future?**

- **Who will our competitors be in the future?**

- **What will our competitive advantage be in the future?**

- **What skills and capabilities will make us unique in the future?**

BUILD A QUALITY TEAM

> *I start with the premise that the function of leadership is to produce more leaders, not more followers.*
>
> Ralph Nader, consumer advocate
> *Time*

Grow the team to enhance the capabilities of your organization. Encourage your team to realize that 1 + 1 = 3. That is, the power, the know-how of each individual is greatly increased when it becomes part of the team. Provide support and unwavering assistance. Share your power. Build and sustain trust.

- *Assemble* your team with specific organizational goals in mind if they are to be a problem solving group. *Train* them. *Disseminate information* to enable top performance.

- *Communicate* their progress to other sectors of the organization. It maintains momentum.

- *Celebrate* their successes. Acknowledge and reward effort and victory. Support disappointments.

In *"Get Better or Get Beaten"*, Jack Welch, CEO of GE sums it up.

"My job," he says *"is to put the best people on the biggest opportunities and the best allocation of dollars in the right places. That's about it. Transfer ideas and allocate resources and get out of the way."*

INNOVATE • IMPROVE • INFLUENCE

Innovation blooms in environments where the work is stimulating, where there are enough resources to develop the innovation, where encouragement is found at all levels. Rubbermaid Inc., with Wolfgang Schmitt at the helm, is an excellent example, since 90 percent of its new products are successful, whereas the American average is 10 percent.

Innovation flounders in environments where the workload is extreme, productivity is closely monitored, and the corporate culture is anti-innovative, due to internal friction, critical attitudes or destructive competition.

What do you do to stimulate innovation? What do you do to impede it?

Innovation involves risk. Be a good risk taker by gathering as much relevant information and data as possible before you begin. The more you know, the smaller the risk. Look for new opportunities and inspire your people to see them as possible.

Strive for improvement that is driven by and for the benefit of your customers. (Always keep in mind that as a leader, you have internal customers—*your employees*—as well). Things can only get better or worse. They never remain the same. Acknowledge quality. Celebrate improvement. Recognize progress. Make tomorrow better for your customers, for your organization, for yourself.

Ask and answer, **am I improving as a leader? Is my organization getting better?**

> *Failing organizations are usually overmanaged and under-led.*
>
> Warren G. Bennis, distinguished university professor and author
> University of Southern California
> *University of Maryland Symposium*

> *——and to be strong, so that those who depend on us may draw strength from our example.*
>
> Rose Kennedy, Mother of John F. Kennedy

"Why should someone do business with me...rather than someone else?"

Over the years, I have asked seminar participants to jot down the characteristics and the skills of the most motivating leaders they had ever had.

Read their comments and ask yourself how many of the remarks can be made about you.

TOP 25 CHARACTERISTICS & SKILLS OF LEADERS

1. A great listener. She really listened to me and my ideas.

2. Believed in me. Respected my ability to do the job.

3. Delegated responsibility well.

4. Came in smiling. Always enthusiastic.

5. Complimented me on my achievements. Gave me credit when I deserved it.

6. Always asked how I was. Interested in me as a person as well as a typist.

7. Was willing to share ideas. An excellent teacher. Ready to teach new skills to make the process better.

8. Criticized the job, not me. Told me both the good and the bad.

9. Her word was her word. A promise made was a promise kept.

10. He wasn't a phony. What you saw was who he was.

Speak softly and carry a big carrot.

Howard C. Lauer, assistant Executive VP
United Jewish Appeal Federation,
Greater Washington, D.C.

---

11. Realized there was more than one way to do a job, so he let each of us do it the way that was best for us, as long as it got done correctly and on time.

> *A great leader sees his people not only as they are, but as they can grow to be.*
>
> Sam Geist

12. Could keep a secret. He was like my dad. I could talk to him.

13. Showed me I was important and my job was important to the company. Made me feel like a somebody.

14. Laid his cards on the table. No hidden agenda. I knew exactly what I was supposed to do, so I could do it properly.

15. Made me feel at home on my first day. Took me around to meet everyone and took me for lunch with a couple of the other people.

16. She was very strict, but she was fair.

17. Had an open door policy. Always available to talk.

18. Found the best in each of us. Made everyone feel special and valuable.

19. Even though there is a staff of 80, she always remembered what we had discussed.

20. Ready and willing to hear and try out new ideas. Didn't always defend the status quo.

21. Took the team approach. Led like a coach. Cheered us on. Turned obstacles into challenges.

22. A true professional. Never gossiped or put people down.

23. Always took our side. Never put us down to clients.

24. There were no favorites. Everyone played by the same rules.

25. Practiced what he preached. Was on time, honest and caring. Expected as much from himself as he did from us.

Every morning and every evening an exemplary leader looks in the mirror and says, *today as a catalyst for action I am going to:*

■ *Learn and grow. Become an agent of change.*

■ *Be open and honest. Face reality.*

■ *Share my experiences, my knowledge. Know what's going on locally and globally and act on it.*

■ *Uphold my values and beliefs.*

■ *Advise my colleagues. Assist them to acquire information.*

■ *Empower and reward those around me. Allocate resources to make success possible.*

■ *Implement change by re-structuring, re-shaping, re-inventing and simplifying the organization and its operations.*

■ *Be patient, be understanding. Manage more by managing less.*

■ *Examine and re-examine my goals and my agenda. Be prepared to innovate and initiate change.*

> **The very essence of leadership is [that] you have to have a vision. It's got to be a vision you articulate clearly and forcefully on every occasion. You can't blow an uncertain trumpet.**
>
> Theodore Hesburgh, President
> Notre Dame University
> *Time*

- *Create a vision. Hold onto it. Communicate it to everyone in the organization.*

- *Take risks. Encourage others to take risks.*

- *Be community minded. Make my organization an integral part of the community.*

- *Be a catalyst for action.*

Do you?

ASK. ANSWER. PLAN. CHANGE

- **ASK** tough questions. Ask them of yourself. Ask them of others. Ask questions that lead to discovery—to renewal—to growth.

- **ANSWER** the questions honestly. Regard them from several perspectives. Crystallize your answers.

- **PLAN** based on those answers. Create a flexible, viable, exciting, stimulating realistic plan. Get your people involved and committed to the plan.

- **CHANGE** to be in sync with your plan. Change to be better—to be sharper—to be light years ahead. Instigate change throughout your organization—make it sharper—make it light years ahead.

> *As for the best leaders, the people do not notice their existence. The next best, the people honor and praise. The next, the people fear and the next, the people hate.*
>
> Lao-Tzu, (604 - 531 B.C.), Chinese philosopher and founder of Taoism

"Why should someone do business with you...rather than someone else?"

ASK. ANSWER. PLAN. CHANGE.

Begin to hone your leadership skills by asking and answering these 21 questions.

1. Why should someone do business with you...rather than someone else?

_____

_____

_____

_____

2. As a leader, as a catalyst for action what do you stand for? What are your values? Your goals?

_____

_____

_____

_____

3. To whom have you communicated your values, your goals? How?

_____

_____

_____

_____

4. What are your strengths as a leader?
   What is your plan to increase them?

   _____

   _____

   _____

   _____

5. What are your weaknesses as a leader?
   What is your plan to eliminate them?

   _____

   _____

   _____

   _____

6. As a leader, as a catalyst for action, what promises do
   you make? What gifts do you give?

   _____

   _____

   _____

   _____

7. What else can you promise?
   What else can you give?

   _____

   _____

   _____

8. How strong are your communication skills?
   What are you doing to improve them?

_____

_____

_____

9. What opportunities do you create to dialogue
   with your staff? With customers?
   How successful are they?

_____

_____

_____

10. What else can you do to develop outstanding two-way
    communication?

_____

_____

_____

11. From how many different perspectives do you view
    the same situation? Does viewing from different
    perspectives change your response? Why? How?

_____

_____

_____

12. What have you done to ameliorate your risk taking?

_____

_____

_____

_____

_____

13. If your staff were to read "the top 25 characteristics of leaders" on pages 294-296, which ones do you think they would apply to you?

_____

_____

_____

_____

_____

14. Which ones would you like them to apply to you?

_____

_____

_____

_____

15. What are you doing to make that happen?

_____

_____

_____

_____

16. **A boss says, "Go." A leader says, "Let's go."**
    What one important example can you illustrate that
    demonstrates you are a leader rather than just a boss?

_____

_____

_____

17. **How has your role as a leader changed in the last**
    10 years? The last two years? Why?

_____

_____

_____

18. **In what ways have you improved? How do you know?**
    In what ways can you still improve?

_____

_____

_____

19. **When you look at yourself in the morning what do you**
    say to yourself that demonstrates you are a catalyst
    for action — an inspiring leader?

_____

_____

_____

20. What would you like your staff to write on your tombstone as a parting tribute?

_____

_____

_____

_____

21. What are you doing right now to make that happen? What can you do? What will you do?

_____

_____

_____

_____

Write in one additional question you feel is important to you, your

situation as a result of reading this section—*and then answer it.*

Q. _____

_____

_____

_____

_____

A. _____

_____

_____

_____

_____

A Final Word

BEFORE YOU BEGIN, A FINAL WORD

Albert Einstein said, "Imagination requires that we raise new questions, explore new possibilities, regard old problems from a new angle!" So does a successful business.

Asking ***"Why should someone do business with you...rather than someone else?"*** is not a one-time ask-and-answer proposition. It is a challenging process that must be repeated every day. Start now and don't look back! You know change happens. Bend into it so that it doesn't knock you down as it charges by.

> ***The road to success is always under construction.***
> Sam Geist

I was inspired by the proactive comment I read in Dr. Stephen Covey's 1996 *Seven Habits of Highly Effective People Calendar.*

> **"Between stimulus and response is our greatest power— the freedom to choose."**

It smacks of the power we each have to control our own future.

Between the questions I ask and the answers I give lies my own

> **You can fix a bad decision, but you can't fix indecision.**
>
> Sam Geist

power, the opportunity to be *revolutionary—exhilarating—motivating—inspiring—influential—actionable—beneficial.* That power is yours as it is mine.

This book contains 542 questions. That's 542 opportunities to question, to think, to search for solutions. My role is to ask again and yet again, **"Why should someone do business with you...rather than someone else?"** In that way, I hope I assist to stimulate ideas, open doors, suggest viable options that move you forward.

Your role is to use your personal answers to create a step-by-step plan, that begins where you are and ends where you want to be, before you are ready to move forward yet again.

> **Nothing will come of nothing. Dare mighty things.**
>
> William Shakespeare

Finally, I feel it is my responsibility to make recommendations. And I recommend action. Action will assist you accommodate your plans, grow your business, achieve your goals. It leads to fulfillment. My objectives in writing this book have been to stimulate action.

It is now up to you. Re-consider your mission, your goals, your hopes and dreams, your reason for being, *by asking.*

Re-inspect your business strategy, your internal operations, *by asking....*

Re-activate your unique, differentiating customer service strategy *by asking....*

Re-examine your staff policies and incentives *by asking*....

Review your communication techniques *by asking*....

Re-evaluate your technological capabilities *by asking*....

Re-vitalize your leadership skills and acumen *by asking*....

"Why should someone do business with you...rather than someone else?"

ASK. ANSWER. PLAN. CHANGE.

Sam Geist

Sam Geist offers:

- customized keynotes, workshops and seminar presentations

- consulting

- facilitating

- video and audio series of all programs

For more information about Sam Geist, his services or to inquire about quantity book orders:

Call 1-800-567-1861 or e-mail samgeist@geistgroup.com

Visit Sam Geist's site on the World Wide Web:

http://www.samgeist.com

Index